MALORUM SECURUS NIHIL TIMEBO

*Simon Greenwood*

# THE CHEVIOT RANTER

*Also by R. W. F. Poole*

Hunting: An Introduction

A Backwoodsman's Year

The Rustic Scribe

Arthur James and I

# THE CHEVIOT RANTER

R. W. F. Poole

*Illustrations by Reginald Bass*

MICHAEL JOSEPH
LONDON

MICHAEL JOSEPH LTD

Published by the Penguin Group
Penguin Books Ltd, 27 Wrights Lane, London W8 5TZ, England
Penguin Books USA Inc., 375 Hudson Street, New York, New York 10014, USA
Penguin Books Australia Ltd, Ringwood, Victoria, Australia
Penguin Books Canada Ltd, 10 Alcorn Avenue, Toronto, Ontario, Canada M4V 3B2
Penguin Books (NZ) Ltd, 182–190 Wairau Road, Auckland 10, New Zealand

Penguin Books Ltd, Registered Offices: Harmondsworth, Middlesex, England

First published in Great Britain 1993

Typeset by Datix International Limited, Bungay, Suffolk
Printed in England by Clays Ltd, St Ives PLC
Filmset in $11\frac{1}{2}$ on $12\frac{1}{2}$ pt Monophoto Palatino

A CIP catalogue record for this book is available from the British Library

ISBN 0 7181 3688 8

The moral right of the author has been asserted

The author and publishers would like
to thank the *Spectator* for permission
to use the copyright article in chapter 16.

All other articles in this book appeared in the *Daily Telegraph*,
*Sunday Telegraph* or *Sunday Telegraph* magazine between January
1990 and April 1992.

# CONTENTS

|   | Introduction | vii |
|---|---|---|
| 1 | Sense and Sensibility | 1 |
| 2 | Have You Heard the One about the Parson, the Rottweiler and the Kennel Club? | 3 |
| 3 | Eggs and Currie Sauce | 7 |
| 4 | Who Is Suited for Farming? | 10 |
| 5 | Trials of a Metropolitan Peasant | 13 |
| 6 | The Finer Points of Spring | 16 |
| 7 | Of Lambs and Cocks and Young Man's Fancy | 19 |
| 8 | The Travels of a Pinstriped Pom | 21 |
| 9 | That Drotted Pond | 27 |
| 10 | The Market on the Smoothfield | 30 |
| 11 | Charley, Matt and Willy Meet Peat | 33 |
| 12 | Of Back Ends, Boche and Bureaucrats | 36 |
| 13 | A Wild Life in Yorkshire | 39 |
| 14 | Of Hills, Ham Sandwiches and Paratroopers | 42 |
| 15 | 'Istha Gannin' t'Show Like?' | 45 |
| 16 | Les Scoots | 52 |
| 17 | First Catch Your Mink | 55 |
| 18 | 'When I Showed Her the Works of My Threshing Machine' (Trad.) | 58 |
| 19 | Sermons in Stones | 61 |
| 20 | Hares, Pheasants and Guns in Suffolk | 64 |
| 21 | Clearances: Old and New | 67 |
| 22 | No One Can Tell Weather, or No | 70 |
| 23 | Of Course It's Pure Coincidence, But . . . | 73 |
| 24 | Of Watching the Lady, Your Wallet and Your Back | 76 |
| 25 | In which the Burra Sahib Muses on Travel and Bathes an Elephant | 79 |
| 26 | Christmas Comes But Once a Year | 85 |

| | | |
|---|---|---|
| 27 | 'It's Really Much the Same in France' | 88 |
| 28 | Driving a Four-Horsepower Bowman | 98 |
| 29 | A Horse Called Nunnington | 102 |
| 30 | Poison, Problems and Good Intentions | 108 |
| 31 | Hounds Across the Border | 110 |
| 32 | The Clean Boot | 113 |
| 33 | In which Politics and Fingers May Both Be Grubby | 116 |
| 34 | Of Bucks and Bothies | 119 |
| 35 | Of Does and Fools and Double-breasted Guns | 122 |
| 36 | Weaving a Story | 125 |
| 37 | Kippers and Corbie Crows | 128 |
| 38 | Trees, Trusts and William-the-Conqueror | 131 |
| 39 | Spring, Sheep Sense and Political Stupidity | 134 |
| 40 | A Boaring Matter | 137 |
| 41 | Board Stiff | 140 |
| 42 | Fish Farmers Have Big Mussels | 144 |
| 43 | A Topping End to a Load of Rubbish | 147 |
| 44 | Can Quangoroos Sing? | 150 |
| 45 | A Rare Sight Indeed | 153 |
| 46 | Of Lambs and Hounds and Nappies | 156 |
| 47 | Life on the Frontier | 159 |
| 48 | Let's Stalk a Rambler in Green Wellies | 162 |
| 49 | John Peel Lives, O.K.? | 165 |
| 50 | Just Ratching About in Four-Wheel Drive | 171 |
| 51 | 'Neck, Knees and Nuts' | 174 |
| 52 | Woods, Wizz and Grass Parks | 177 |
| 53 | The Political Correctness of Zapping Grey Squirrels | 180 |
| 54 | The Stirring Tale of Jonathan Brock and the Women's Institute | 183 |
| 55 | Indian Clubs Come Up Trumps | 186 |
| 56 | An Organic Rumour about Diversification | 196 |
| 57 | Problems in the Borders, at the Bottom of the Year | 200 |
| 58 | *La France Profonde* | 203 |
| 59 | Coarse Shooting | 206 |
| 60 | Cider Unaided, by M Delors | 209 |
| 61 | Twenty-four Hours at the Savoy | 212 |
| 62 | Country Law | 225 |
| | Index | 229 |

# INTRODUCTION

THE TITLE OF of this book requires a little explanation. 'Cheviot' is fairly straightforward. 'The Cheviot' is England's highest hill (2,500 – Imperial feet, and none of your damned metric nonsense); its long, imposing bulk constitutes the farthest skyline in the view from my little house.

'The Cheviots' are the range of hills that begin almost at the bottom of my farm, and stretch some forty miles to the west and the Cumberland border. For some miles the Anglo/Scottish border ('The Scotch Fence') runs along the crest of the hills. It is a stark and beautiful landscape of 'white grass', heather and rock; of great sweeping hillsides and tumbling hill-streams; a hard land of scattered steadings, few humans and thousand upon thousand of sheep. These hills are the last wild place in England. I hope that this happy state maintains, and that they do not get trampled to death like the poor old Lake District. The prognosis is not good. The main trod up Cheviot itself is twenty yards wider than it was ten years ago, and brightly coloured 'kagools' are much more common than they were a few years ago; if that is possible.

'Cheviot' is also the name of one of the breeds of sheep that have been traditionally bred to cope with the harsh conditions in the hills, and to convert the sparse grazing into some of the most toothsome meat that you will ever eat.

The pronunciation of Cheviot is a tomato/tomayto situation: the burning question is whether to 'Chevviot' or 'Cheeviot'. I asked an old and wise man, who assured me that the latter was correct. The aboriginal inhabitants neatly sidestep the problem by calling it 'Chiviot'. You may please yourselves.

However you may care to pronounce them, it is the Cheviot Hills and the way of life of those who live in and around them, that provide the background and inspiration for the bulk of my scribblings. This way of life reminds me of the days of my youth in the West of England, where it no longer exists; there it has been homogenized, pasteurized, civilized and sub-urbanized out of existence. There is no doubt that we are now well on the way to the happy state where the whole of England south of the River Tyne is going to become one mega suburb populated by Essex-Man clones. Thus will nice Mr Major's dream come true, and we shall become a classless nation, or, more exactly, a nation totally without class.

I very much hope that the Borders will manage to hold out for a bit longer against this disgusting prospect. The hard, heather-bred and independent-minded men of the Borders have a properly cynical appreciation of Political Correctness. They will not be so easily moulded.

'Gosh! he does go on,' I hear you say. 'I suppose that's the Ranting bit. Ranting, that's what he's doing.' *Chambers Dictionary* describes Ranting as: 'declaiming bombastically; to storm; to scold', which is not really my line, whatever people may tell you. But someone has got to stand up for the silent minority of aboriginal countrymen who want to ignore fashionable clap-trap, and be left alone to live their own lives in their own ways. So if I can fight back, just a little, for the Countryman, against those who do 'declaim bombastically' and those who do 'storm' at us and 'scold' us, then I am happy to be classed as a Ranter.

Ranting has happier connotations. The Borders is a great place for traditional music; for singing, piping and fiddling. There is a class of Northumbrian tune called a 'Rant'. *Chambers* defines it as a 'lively tune', which is near enough. My friend Joe Hutton, the famous Northumbrian piper, defines it as 'similar to a reel, but a bit slower time'.

So that is *The Cheviot Ranter*. Anyone who takes exception to anything that is written here may do so with my blessing. I hope that more of you will regard it as a lively tune of words from the Border Hills.

Chapter One

# SENSE AND SENSIBILITY

W<small>E ARE LOSING</small> our senses. We abuse our noses with fumes and noxious substances which deaden our sense of smell. Our hearing is battered by noise: traffic, trannies, trains, planes and politicians. We blur our sight with print, VDUs and continuous artificial light.

The price we pay for our 'civilized' state would seem to be spectacles, hearing aids and sniffles. Sight, smell and hearing are only the stalk of the potato. What other sensory tubers lie buried deep in the dark loam of the mind?

What about Memory? An English officer, attached to the Sultan of Oman's forces, was amazed that an Arab NCO would absorb a string of complicated instructions without ever taking a note. The Arabs have a largely oral culture, and they are therefore quite accustomed to operating a mental filing system.

Many parts of Britain had an oral culture until the old ways were largely destroyed by zealous churchmen and educationalists. However, there are still some well-known traditional musicians who cannot read music, but can carry hundreds of tunes in their heads; can you remember the words of *Nellie Dean*?

In the same tradition are shepherds, who can remember generations of family details relating to their sheep. Fred and I were discussing a ewe with a 'backbody' (cervical prolapse). She had apparently done the same thing two years since on the morning of the hunter trials. 'I would mind that she was out of yon old speckled-face ewe that we drafted last back end (autumn),' said Fred. I minded nothing of the sort, nor any of it, but then I do not come from generations of shepherds who stored all their stock records on a cerebral floppy disc.

There was a recent announcement of some sort of computer-ized in-car navigation system. As I understand it, you have a screen on the dashboard which shows exactly where you are in relation to Acacia Avenue, or wherever. The manufacturers are very pleased with this, but I wonder if we really want people driving about fumbling with their reading spectacles and peering at screens. It is much better to have an in-head navigation system. Many birds and animals have a very highly developed directional sense; as do some 'primitive' people, such as myself.

Telepathy is another sense that has been civilized out of most of us. Dogs make great use of telepathy. No one who has seen two terriers silently shouting at each other across the breadth of a yard: 'To the Rabbits! To the Rabbits! But wait until no one is looking', can doubt that.

All good dog handlers have the gift of telepathic communi-cation with dogs. You might have it. Next time you take your dog for a walk, try *thinking* what you want him to do next and see what happens; if he disappears after the cat from No. 32, then you might do better with a hamster.

Most of us have long since lost our weather sense. Animals know nothing of Bracknell and Nice Mr Fish, but they know when to batten down the hatches. I once lived on Dartmoor, as did a lot of shaggy Galloway cattle. You could always tell when it was going to snow because you would see long, black lines of Galloways coming down off the high moor to seek shelter on the lower ground. I never remember them being wrong.

Many people whose lives are ruled by the weather can feel changes coming. The natives of St Kilda were especially famous as weather prophets. A friend of mine was haymaking with an elderly man who was one of the last St Kildans. It was a glorious summer day with the glass 'set fair'. The St Kildan said it would rain by two o'clock and was laughed at. He was wrong: the deluge came at five past two. I suppose he had got a bit rusty.

# Chapter Two

# HAVE YOU HEARD THE ONE ABOUT THE PARSON, THE ROTTWEILER AND THE KENNEL CLUB?

M Y ROTTWEILER IS called Duncan. He is not yet fully grown, but weighs in at the thick end of 90 lbs. He is also immensely strong. Both size and strength will increase.

Duncan is our second Rottweiler. Like his predecessor he is a gentle dog of immense charm and great intelligence. Over the years I must have handled some hundreds of dogs of different sorts, shapes and sizes. I have no doubt that Duncan is one of the nicest dogs that I have ever known. *But* (and it is a big *but*) I am always aware of the fact that Duncan is a Rottweiler. Rottweilers are guard dogs. That is what they have been bred for for many centuries. The Rottweiler is fiercely loyal to his pack. In Duncan's case his 'pack' is the family Poole. He is very polite to visitors if they are properly introduced and well-behaved. However, were you to come through the window at one o'clock in the morning (even with the good intention of trying to sell me some double glazing) then I think that Duncan would regard you as being out of order: things might not go well for you.

With both our Rottweilers we were aware from the bumbling puppy stage that we were dealing with a very particular type of dog, and all the handling and training was angled accordingly. A combination of great strength and great intelligence has an obvious potential for great virtue. The same combination that has been ill-used or ill-trained can be an accident round the corner.

Rottweilers are victims of greed and fashion. They became macho Status Symbols; a terrible fate for any breed of dog. Greedy breeders cashed in with inferior stock. Some owners should not be put in charge of a teddy bear, let alone 120 lbs of bone, brain and muscle. Many wretched Rottweilers are kept cooped up in tiny flats, or chained up in dreary backyards. They are handled badly, and become brutalized. Very often, because they are stronger and more intelligent than their 'masters', they become the boss of the family pack: then there is trouble ahead.

It is right that people should be concerned about Rottweilers. It is not right that these fine dogs should be damned as a breed. The damnation should be visited on the people who turn their virtue into vice.

From a breed of very large dogs to something much smaller: the Kennel Club is going to recognize the Jack Russell Terrier. To be more exact (if I have understood things correctly), the Kennel Club is going to recognize the 'Parson Jack Russell Terrier' as a 'variant' of the Fox Terrier.

There is no doubt that the Kennel Club is an organization packed to the gunwales with worthy and well-meaning people, but the Kennel Club means Dog Shows, and this is where the doubts may creep in. The showing of dogs is not a bad thing in itself. Dog Shows can be fun and a jolly day out, but that is all they should be. Anyone who has ever judged at a Dog Show will testify that showing can often arouse the baser sort of human passions; especially if the judging has upset a well-laden applecart.

I am against dogs being bred just for showing. The Dog Show world is terribly susceptible to fashion. Breeders then alter the dog to fit the fashion. This seems to lead inevitably to the physical deterioration of the breed concerned. Exaggeration, you may say. Exactly that, I will reply. See what exaggeration has done to the Bulldog, for an instance. There is no more bull baiting, but the Bulldog should at least look as though it would be up to the job; it does not seem to be able to do much except wheeze these days. It would also be hard to imagine the modern show Bloodhound tracking much more than its dinner.

Many breeds of dog have become grotesques because of showing fashions and human vanity. It would indeed be a shame if such a fate were to overtake the Jack Russell.

What is a Parson Jack Russell Terrier anyway? Parson Russell was a Victorian clergyman in North Devon with a passion for foxhunting. He kept his own pack of hounds in the teeth of determined opposition from his Bishop. He also bred his own Earth Dogs (terrier merely being a Frenchified way of saying the same thing), to evict foxes from their holes. That was, and is, the work of the terrier.

There was no motor transport in those far-off days. Men, hounds and horses hacked to the meet (sometimes as much as twenty miles), did their day's hunting and rode home. The terriers would be expected to do the same. This meant that the Parson's terriers were long on the leg, tough as hobnailed boots and sharp as razors.

There is one point that is important to understand: the Parson never attempted to establish a Breed of terrier. He was interested only in a Type that would do his work. He just bought any good, working terrier that looked to be the right sort, and which his wallet would run to. I have seen pictures of some of the Parson's terriers, and from time to time I have had terriers from one of the strains that he thought a lot of.

The Rev Russell got many of his terriers from the Williams family of Scorrier in Cornwall, where they bred their own excellent strain of terrier for many years. The 'Scorrier' terrier was very much a Type. They were leggy terriers, rough-coated with undocked tails, immensely tough and charming, and would run with hounds. This may give some idea of the Type favoured by Parson Russell. To know more what a 'Parson Jack Russell Terrier' should look like, what better than the Parson's own description of his famous Trump:

   ... The coat, which is thick, close and a trifle wiry, is
   well calculated to protect the body from wet and cold. ..
   The legs are straight as arrows, the feet perfect: the

loins and conformation of the whole frame indicative of hardihood and endurance; while the size and height of the animal may be compared to that of a full grown vixen fox.

Today the term 'Jack Russell Terrier' seems to cover a multitude of sins that include 'Chippendale' legs, barrel chests and backs so long that a central jockey wheel is needed. I just hope that the Kennel Club will at least pay the old Gentleman the compliment of ensuring that the terriers that bear his name look something like the original.

# Chapter Three

# EGGS AND CURRIE SAUCE

WHAT SORT OF eggs do you like? Do you prefer nice, fresh, farmyard eggs with lovely brown shells? You may be very lucky to taste any of that sort in the Britain of the future.

I expect you all remember when Ms Edwina Currie went to work on an egg and finished up with it splattered all over her political career. The eggs rebounded into the lap of Nice Mr Gummer, who promptly went into spasm with political Salmonella. The result of that spasm is that it is now becoming increasingly difficult to buy proper free-range eggs.

I eat my own eggs when they are available and when I can find the blessed things: game hens are very clever at hiding their nests. When we had no home eggs it used to be my pleasant custom to go to Mrs Sharps' Good Life Shop in Wooler. Mrs Sharp used to have baskets of big, fresh farm eggs displayed on the shop counter. The basket of hens' eggs is no longer there. The Men from the Ministry have decreed that, under the Testing of Poultry Flocks Order 1989, eggs from battery hens may be displayed in a basket: free-range eggs may not. The object of this ruling is to 'protect the consumer'.

The TPFO also states that if you sell eggs for human consumption then your flock has to be monitored for evidence of Salmonella. You do this by taking what the Ministry coyly refers to as a 'cloacal swab', which you send to a laboratory for testing. The producer pays for the testing. The farmer whose flock numbers from 500 to umpteen thousand has to test a sample of sixty birds every twelve weeks. Should your flock number twenty-five, or less, then you have to test the lot. This means that thousands of birds kept in battery cages, where the risk of infection might be thought to be highest, are never tested at all.

What does this mean for the small farmyard producer? It means that the cost of testing his few free-range hens is likely to be the same as for the intensive producer with many thousands of caged birds. As a result of this many small producers have gone out of business. Over one million British hens have been slaughtered, and a large proportion of the eggs you are now eating are imports. Only a small percentage of these imports are tested. They are not exactly newly laid.

You might think that all this is grossly unfair, and represents a bureaucratic victimization of the small enterprisers: the very sort of people that the present government is supposed to be so keen on. The Ministry's position was lucidly presented in 1989 by Mr R. Lowson, Head of Animal Health Division.

> With regard to the sampling costs incurred, the number of samples required has been established on advice from the State Veterinary Service in accordance with standard statistical methods designed to achieve ninety-five per cent probability of detecting salmonella infection. So while the number of samples necessary is proportionally higher for a smaller flock this only offers the same statistical chance of detecting infection as for a larger flock.

I hope that that is now clear to all of you.

It did not seem very clear, or fair, to Mrs Sharp. She got up a petition, dressed up as a chicken, and arrived at the Ministry of Agriculture on the back of a motorbicycle to hand in her protest. This aroused some press interest. A picture of Mrs Sharp, with a basket of eggs on her counter, appeared in the *Daily Telegraph*. A copy of this same article and picture landed in Leeds and on the desk of Mr Sweeting, the Regional Egg Marketing Inspector. It seems that there was an arrow pointing to the basket of eggs and a little Ministry memo asking what he was doing about it?

This might be construed as a crude attempt to put the frighteners on someone who was ruffling the dignity of the Ministry. In fact Mrs Sharp says that Mr Sweeting was terribly nice and helpful. He suggested that they could overcome their problem by turning the whole of the back of their tiny shop into a licensed packing station. He was also helpful about the cloacal swabs. It is apparently just as acceptable to provide a faeces sample from each bird: what could be simpler?

There the matter rests. However, there are still fresh eggs in baskets on the counter of the Good Life Shop in Wooler. Duck, goose, quail, gleany and bantam eggs are not covered by the TPFO. I wonder if Mr Sweeting will be getting another memo (and a copy of this article) from Nice Mr Gummer.

# Chapter Four

# WHO IS SUITED FOR FARMING?

A CCORDING TO THE NFU there were 100,000 part-time farmers in the UK in 1989. Part-time farming is on the increase as more farmers are forced to seek another source of income. This is hardly surprising when you consider the current state of British Agriculture. I know that the MAFF claim that farm incomes rose by eleven per cent last year. I telephoned the Ministry to ask it how it had arrived at this figure. The Ministry was very coy about producing its calculations for inspection, so we must accord this figure the respect due to all John Selwyn Gummer's statements: he is a pillar of the Church of England, after all. All I know is that my farm income has not risen by eleven per cent; in fact it has not risen at all; it has been falling steadily. It would be nice to say that costs have fallen in sympathy, but they march inexorably upwards.

The question is what to do about it? One of my problems is that my farm is very small. At one time I considered investing in more land and more stock. This would have meant borrowing money and trusting the politicians not to move the goalposts again. No farmer should have any faith in politicians; even if they are members of the General Synod. I will invest no more money in agriculture at the moment. So I have done what many others are doing: I have got myself a job and become a part-time farmer.

Part-time farmers do not necessarily farm small acreages, but the economics of scale mean that the smaller operator is more likely to have to seek additional income. In the days before they became dormitories for yuppies, most villages would have had a screen of smallholdings around them. These little farms would not have been of sufficient size for a man to work full-time, but they did provide a valuable addition to the family income and to the family table.

The smallholding would carry poultry, pigs, probably a few sheep and almost certainly a house cow. I remember a village where the 'cow keepers' would turn their cows out into the wide, grass-verged street in the morning. The cows would make their way down to the pond at the bottom of the village and then graze their way home. The grass is now all mown within an inch of its life, and the modern 'villagers' would have the vapours if they met a cow in the street. As for cow pats in the road, oh dear me no: might dirty a green welly.

The other part of the 'part-time' varied. Some men worked for the council on the roads. My old friend Les was one of the best men to lean on a shovel that Barsetshire County Council ever employed, but his heart and soul were with his pigs on the immaculate smallholding behind his little thatched cottage. The local post office and shop could be combined with a bit of farming. There was the man on Dartmoor who did a daily post round of the scattered moorland farms on his shepherding pony.

Many old-fashioned publicans combined the purveying of beer and spirits with a smallholding. It is sad to relate that this old-fashioned type of publican is now an endangered species, along with the old-fashioned public house. They are being drowned in a swamp of bogus horse-brasses and retired majors of equally dubious provenance.

The 'Squarson', who cured his own bacon as well as souls, has totally disappeared to the best of my knowledge and belief. This is a great pity. Such men had knowledge of the practical problems of their rural parishioners. It would not hurt the modern Church of England if it got a few calluses on its hands and a few muscles on its Christianity.

Along with the lorry drivers, quarrymen and agricultural contractors, there are now many part-time farmers in the ranks of commerce and the professions. It is true that many of them approached farming from the other end of the spectrum: that is, they made some money first and then buried part of it in a farm.

So we part-time farmers are a mixed bunch; probably as

varied as the products of our holdings. I suspect that the thing that we all have in common is a deep love of farming and a determination to stay with it. There is also the interesting dichotomy between two different sorts of work. Sir Winston Churchill regarded a change of work as being the best form of relaxation. This piece is being written in the small hours of the morning, between visits to the lambing shed. I am not so sure about the relaxation bit.

Chapter Five

# TRIALS OF A METROPOLITAN PEASANT

I WAS SITTING IN a taxi and a Knightsbridge traffic jam when I saw one: they really do stick out like an inflamed digit in the London crowds. This one was a 'He'un'. His shoes were highly polished and his suit offered no concessions to current fashion fads: it is a guinea to a gooseberry that the suit smelled of mothballs, and had belonged to the chap's father. The two great betrayers of his provenance were his walk and his face. He strode the pavements with that long, slack-kneed stride that is more suited to the slopes of Shillmoor than to the pavements of Central London. But the face, that was the thing. The face was that marvellous brick red with purply overtones that can only be achieved by thirty years' exposure to wind, weather and not a little whisky. This colouring would cease abruptly just above the eyebrows where the hat band comes. The forehead, hidden under the felt hat, would be fish-belly white. I know, because my face is exactly the same. It takes one to know one, and I know a Countryman come to Town when I see one.

True Countrymen do not go to London (or any other town) promiscuously. They require some pretty heavy reason for going: as it might be buying an Old Etonian tie, visiting the man of business or bringing about the downfall of the government. Not, I hasten to add, that you are likely to find your True Countryman taking part in a weekend political rally: that might mean missing a day's hunting. Anyway, he probably thinks that the Anarchists are a Rugby Football team and much too hearty to mix with.

None of this should be construed as 'going shopping'. Countrymen only make their purchases at places where the nice man rubs his hands and asks, 'Shall we have it sent round, sir?' Countrymen may carry bags of dead rabbits at home, but they do not carry packets in London.

The place 'it' is likely to be sent round to is the Club. Now there are clubs in London and then there are clubs. Most countrymen have access to the sort of club where they can snore off their luncheon in a large leather armchair, secure in the knowledge that the hall-porter will defend them to the death against intrusions from wives, mistresses and any other social flotsam.

I once dined with a friend at this sort of club and he said why did we not go on to his other club? Well why not? The other club was very dark and smoky. The male clientele seemed to be all very large, swarthy and designer-stubbled. In spite of the murk, they all wore dark glasses. My friend was obviously very popular: I mean we were absolutely besieged by very jolly young ladies. I was rather taken with a lovely Austrian girl, and suggested that we might sneak off for a cup of cocoa. 'I vill cost you £140,' she said, 'but don' vorry, I vill have myself put on your friend's bill.' You do not get that sort of service in Toller Porcorum.

There are other hot places in London. In fact everything in London is far too hot. No one should be allowed to heat their buildings to more than fifty degrees. This would save Finite Fossil Fuels and make Urbans far more healthy. They would also wear more wool, which would be good for my farming. I can see the slogan: 'Wear woollen combinations: your ozone friendly layer'.

Travelling to, from and in London is a nightmare. I used to be a confirmed railway enthusiast, but no more. British Railways have finally crushed my spirit. I have sat in a broken-down train outside Peterborough once too often, and Kings Cross must be the world's nastiest station. I now fly to Heathrow, and I must say that Lord King has not half brassed-up British Airways. Here is the rub: it can take longer to get from Heathrow to Central London than it does to get from Newcastle to Heathrow. It is complete nonsense that there is no proper way of connecting the nation's premier aerodrome with its premier city.

I tried the tube on one occasion. It is probably a good thing to get your first impression of London from London Transport. On the merry Piccadilly line you will get a quick induction course in overheating, overcrowding, oversneezing and the London Charm of Manner. You will experience the exquisite pleasure of sitting outside Acton Town for twenty minutes ('operational difficulties'). You can then experience the total failure of London Transport's Customer Relations training. All I got from the experience was late, and a raging throat infection. So it is back to the taxis and the cheerful home-spun philosophizing from your standard, cheerful, cheeky, cuddly cabby.

The discerning Countryman will arrive with a deep sigh of relief at The Savoy Hotel. London's best hotel is a haven of peace and slightly quirky excellence, where town-ravaged tissues may be pleasantly restored.

Very few Rurals will know their Muswell Hill from their Arnos Grove. They will know a fairly small area west of Piccadilly Circus. It is here that they tend to buy their shirts and the shoes with toe caps that they will lovingly polish. Somewhere here they are likely to have their suits built when the inherited ones finally fall apart or unplanned development has taken place ('More corpse, more cloth, sir'). Here they will come to buy hats and watch with fascinated horror the foreign gentleman in white shoes, dark suit and orange shirt trying on a red-and-white-checked deerstalker hat.

After such a shock our Countryman might be found pensively sitting in the spring sunshine in the park, lining up shots at pigeons with his umbrella and wishing that he was home with his dogs and his sheep. There is, he tells himself, nothing wrong with London that would not be solved by ploughing the whole place up and putting it down to grass.

# Chapter Six

# THE FINER POINTS OF SPRING

THE ORIGINAL POINT-to-points took place at the end of the hunting season. The participants would assemble at Point A in full hunting rig, riding the horses which they had hunted all season. They would then race across country to Point B: from Point-to-Point. In those far-off days there were no made courses. The riders took their own line across the intervening country, jumping whatever horrifying obstacles might be the speciality of that particular area. It might be stone walls in the Cotswolds or earth banks in the West Country. In the great grazing grounds that then made up the English Midlands they would have to cope with all the various permutations of the thorn fence from the newly cut and laid 'Stake and Bound' through to the 'Bullfinch', by way of the 'Double Oxer'. This particularly nasty obstacle was a cut-and-laid fence with a ditch on both sides. To keep the cattle out of the ditch there would be a split oak 'ox rail' on the outside of each ditch: an oxer. It was deemed impossible to jump twelve consecutive double oxers without getting a crumpling fall: 'cutting an arser' as it was delicately known.

From these somewhat rough-and-ready beginnings things began to smooth out a bit. The point-to-point became a social occasion as well as a race. Spectators did not reckon too much to having the race disappear into the distance, and so circular, laid-out courses became the thing. The natural fences began to give way to artificial brush fences.

As the courses became faster and more sophisticated so did the horses and the owners. This prompted the Jockey Club to take a more professional interest in the conduct of hunt racing and lay a regulation or two on the organizers. Today a point-to-point may only be held by an 'A Hunt, or two or more adjoining hunts, being Foxhounds, Deerhounds, Harriers (Masters being Members of their respective Associations)': everybody quite clear about that? The exceptions to this rule are Her Majesty's Armed Forces.

In case you should feel so inspired at this stage that you wish to rush out, buy a horse and have a crack at point-to-pointing, just pause for a moment. It is not as simple as that. Your horse has to be 'qualified' with a particular hunt; this means that it has to be the property of a Member of, Subscriber to, or Farmer in, a particular hunt. The horse must have been hunted during the current hunting season and have a certificate to say so. The certificate used to include the words 'regularly and fairly hunted', a phrase which caused more than its fair share of problems. The modern point-to-point horse is a highly bred, expensive and specialized animal. This type of horse is ill-suited to many modern hunting countries. Point-to-point horses are no longer expected to jump four feet of solid, wire-festooned timber out of hock-deep plough.

What about *your* qualifications as the rider? To get your Rider's Certificate, you too have to be a Member, Subscriber or Farmer in a hunt, or a Serving Member of HM Forces.

This is a simplified summary. The Jockey Club regulations for Point-to-Point Steeplechases are the size of a small novel. You may read them for yourself without fear of encountering sex or violence.

Those who attend point-to-points may be roughly divided into two categories: those who go for the racing and those who do not. The racing category is the smaller one, so let us start there. Point-to-pointing is an amateur sport, but it arouses great intensity of feeling amongst its devotees. The prize money is peanuts, but it is not unknown for the odd shilling to be wagered. Some of them can be very odd shillings indeed.

Once upon a time there was a man who entered a little mare for a point-to-point. She was known to be very fast over a shortish distance, but would not stay the three-mile trip; she was very long odds. At the two-mile mark she was leading the field by some twenty lengths. At this point the course turned through a double gateway in a large bank. As soon as the mare was through the gap, a man in a ragged mackintosh appeared out of a ditch, closed the double gates in the face of the oncoming field, padlocked them and faded into the vegetation. The little mare won in a canter.

For most people the point-to-point is a great social occasion. It will attract all sorts and conditions of people, many of whom would never think of going to a pukka race meeting or going hunting. I am minded of one rabidly anti-hunting man who adored point-to-points. It never occurred to him that he was contributing to the finances of the local hunt. People go for the pleasure of their cars sinking to the axles in muddy car parks. They love eating soggy sandwiches out of the car boot, whilst the rain seeps relentlessly into every nook and cranny. They are braced by the wind that comes whipping in off the North Sea. Then there is the fun of trying to get Daddy out of the beer tent before he starts climbing the tent pole yet again.

You can donate your money to the bookies.

You can lose your green wellies in the mud.

You can be ridden over by a sweating, foam-flecked, point-to-pointer and, if you really get lucky, you might even be kicked by his horse as well.

It will all be the greatest fun and a great day out. There is bound to be a point-to-point somewhere near you today, so gird up your loins and go. I wish you all a very jolly day.

# Chapter Seven

# OF LAMBS AND COCKS AND YOUNG MAN'S FANCY

IT IS QUITE certain that I have written about Spring before, but then, you see, it comes round every year in some shape or form and cannot be denied or ignored; not, at least, by those whose lives are ruled by the seasons and the weather.

There often comes a period of false spring in February: days of soft, greasy warmth. In this treacherous period misguided trees throw out a bud or two and the odd crocus may pop its head above the parapet. A nasty shock usually awaits those lulled by Nature's apparently relaxed mood. Those who witter on about 'getting back to Nature' seldom realize what a bloody-minded old bitch she can be. Nature seldom lets spring pass without loading her handbag with something heavy and laying about her. The innocent and incautious are likely to catch it right behind the ear.

Spring is not always apparent in the Borders. You know it ought to be spring from the calendar, but often it is just winter with longer days. I judge the coming of spring from the birds. There comes the wild, plaintive piping of the curlews. The peewits wheel and whistle over the farm, and the oyster catchers are back on the river.

Then there are the game fowl. I have a large population of semi-wild game fowl. The cocks are Black-Breasted Light Reds for those who are interested. I never interfere with them and they form their own social structure in and around the sheep shed. Ginger is the boss cock. He has appropriated most of the hens and has the stable yard and the top end of the shed for his territory. Lomax rules a lesser harem at the bottom of the shed. I do not bother to name the lesser cocks until it is plain whether they are going to survive or not. The cocks mark the advent of spring with a sudden surge of rape and grievous bodily harm. This is indeed nature red in beak and claw. Ginger is no democrat. He maintains his rule by mayhem and murder: that is the way of Nature.

'In the spring a young man's fancy lightly turns to thoughts of . . .': lambing, ploughing, discing, harrowing, sowing and one hundred other jobs; not too much time for romance. The earth may move for you, but it is likely to be whilst on a tractor, if you see what I mean.

Our fore-elders were made of sterner stuff. I am minded of Roger, the plough boy. Roger was coming home over the Down, sitting sideways on old Dobbin, when he met with Pretty Bessie the Milkmaid. It may be that they discovered a mutual interest in the poetry of Alfred, Lord Tennyson; whatever, they deemed it right to have a deep and meaningful discussion about something. Dobbin might have hindered the conversation, and there was nothing to tie him to on the open Down, so Roger tethered him to his ankle.

Perhaps Dobbin was not keen on poetry, or perhaps he just wanted his tea. For whatever reason, at a crucial moment in the young couple's discussion, Dobbin set out for home and, things being what they were, Roger went too. He no doubt remarked to himself that 'parting is such sweet sorrow'. I think that it took the spring out of his fancy anyway.

## Chapter Eight

# THE TRAVELS OF A PINSTRIPED POM

THE ONE THING you do not want to be in New Zealand is 'up yourself'. In case you are wondering about the interesting mechanics of this operation, let me hastily explain that it is an expression indicating pomposity. Most New Zealanders believe that most Britons (hereinafter referred to as 'Poms') have built-in pomposity.

I recently travelled to New Zealand as a guest of the New Zealand Hunts' Association and the Hawkes Bay Hunt Centenary Celebrations Committee, which you might think would be enough to make any Pom pompous. However, thirty-six hours of continuous travelling tends to take the starch out of most people, even after the cheerful ministrations of Air New Zealand. All Air NZ Captains preface their announcements with: 'Ladies and Gentlemen, Boys and Girls', which helps to set the tone.

Any starch that might still have survived as I staggered out of the customs hall at Auckland was dispelled by the greeting: 'A big, red-faced Pom with a Mo (moustache): you must be Willy Poole.' Ray and Mary Coles had been detailed to look after us (the wife came too) until the further flight on to Napier. The Coles epitomize the instant warmth and friendship that visitors to New Zealand are offered. What the visitors do with it subsequently is up to them.

Rural New Zealanders work extremely hard. They also play very hard. The Horse still rules rural life. In spite of motor-bicycles, horses are still a vital part of the work force on most big cattle and sheep stations. They are also used for leisure:

racing, polo, show jumping and hunting are all considered to be essential ingredients of a properly balanced lifestyle; along with Rugby Football, of course.

There are thirty hunts in New Zealand. Every four years they hold a National Hound Show in a different part of the country. This time the Hawkes Bay Hunt, who are in the middle of the North Island, were the hosts. As it was also the HBH centenary year, they had planned a week of celebrations around the Hound Show, which included five days hunting, barbecues, dances and very little sleep. More than 500 people had brought their horses from all over the two islands with the serious intention of making whoopee. What better chance for a stranger to get to know the natives and their country.

The New Zealand Hunts' Association had invited me to judge this particular National Hound Show. I understand that I am the first Briton to be accorded this honour. I was not backward in letting this fact loose (very casually, you understand) amongst my friends. Their reactions fell neatly into two categories. There were those who said: 'You mean they are flying you all the way to New Zealand to judge a Hound Show? Gosh, you must be an absolutely *super* judge.' The other lot sniggered and said: 'Well, no one will have you to judge in this country anymore. You really screwed up when you judged in America last year. I suppose New Zealanders have not sussed you out yet: poor blighters.' Which lot were right? You must ask the Kiwis.

A warning to air travellers concerns Bowler Hats. I was under orders to wear British Hound Judge's No. 1 dress for the show. This consists of bowler hat, stiff collar, London suit and town shoes ('toe caps will be highly polished'). The transportation of a bowler hat half-way round the world is not without problems. All security men seem to be convinced that a boxed bowler must be made out of Semtex.

There were 200 hounds to be judged, once I was neatly embowlered at the show. It was a long day in soaring temperatures. I steamed gently and wished that Security had confiscated the wretched Hat.

The whole thing was a triumph of organization for the

HBH. Representatives of all thirty NZ hunts had brought their horses, and in the case of some of the South Island people this had meant a four-day drive. Accommodation was arranged for 200 hounds, 500 horses, and I do not know how many people.

New Zealand is a country of great and various beauty. You are never far away from the mountains or the sea. As the population is only 3.5 million there are few problems of space. The New Zealanders appreciate their country and like you to appreciate it too. When you do, their charming response is: 'It's wonderful to have it and wonderful to share it with you.'

Hawkes Bay is an area of rolling grass hills, not unlike Northumberland. It is home to many old-established farming families who hacked their farms out of the 'bush' and have hung in there through boom and bust, drought and plenty. The same applies to much of the New Zealand farming community. This makes them tough, practical and determined. Their humour is physical, pithy and up front; totally without irony. They respect stamina in both man and animal. Should you fall on your bum (physically or metaphorically) they expect you to get up, grin and say 'She'll be right'. If you sit there and whine they will notch your ear with their huge shepherding knives and send you to the canning factory (metaphorically, of course). They hate 'bludgers' (scroungers) and 'whingeing' (whining). They consider both conditions to be endemic in modern Britain, and it is difficult not to agree with them.

The first ever meet of the HBH was held at the home of the Groom family, so what better place to hold a celebratory barbecue for all the visitors. The 'Barby' is a great New Zealand tradition, their climate being conducive to outdoor living. It was certainly different to the 'two soggy sausages and beefburger' horror one is sometimes subjected to in Britain. There was venison, beef, sausages, salads, a whole pig on a spit and lots of goodies. The food in New Zealand is superb if you like good meat, vegetables and fruit. The wine is very jolly too: unpretentious, but slurps well.

The Kiwis love dancing and approach it with the vigour

and enthusiasm that they approach all physical activities. Their taste tends towards Country and Western music, but it is the C & W of my youth. It was very nostalgic to meet the *Rock Island Line* and *On Top of Old Smoky* again. What with hunting by day and partying by night the Jet Lag was not getting much of a look in, especially as one of the things the Kiwis are bad about is going to bed: if one person is more or less vertical then the party is deemed to be ongoing.

New Zealanders love speeches and make them on every possible occasion. On the night after the show they had a sit-down dinner for 650 people and quite a lot of speeches, including one from me. I am terrified by speechifying, but as I lurched to my feet, my lovely neighbour leant over and whispered: 'Give 'em a bit of smut: they'll like that.' This is very good advice for anyone contemplating antipodean public speaking. I have to say that the Kiwis are a wonderful audience: if you feel lousy when you stand up, you will sit down feeling that you are the best thing since rare roast beef; especially as they are prone to singing 'For he's a jolly good fellow' with very little provocation. The New Zealanders are lusty singers once started, but I was sad to discover that they do not appear to have any traditional songs of their own. I had hoped to enlarge my repertoire.

You will meet no more friendly or hospitable people than the Kiwis; as long as you are not 'up yourself'. How did I do? Well, I started as the 'Pinstriped Pom' and finished as 'Dog Tucker Willy': you must judge for yourselves.


What is Ngamatea (nah mah tee yah)? It is Romance and Pragmatism and Adventure and one of the most beautiful places you ever will see. Ngamatea is a farm. At one time it covered 250,000 acres and was the biggest farm in New Zealand. At 3,000 feet and over, it is also one of the highest.

Travel west from the rolling, fertile grasslands of Hawkes Bay, on the east coast of New Zealand's North Island, and you will be confronted by the bush-covered crags of the central mountain range that forms the country's spine. The tar seal gives way to a dirt road that corkscrews and hairpins through this forbidding country. You may be forgiven for hoping that you do not meet a heavily laden road-train on one of the precipitous bends of the notorious Gentle Annie Hill.

Some seventy miles into the Ranges the traveller emerges on to a high rolling plateau, an expanse of brown, wind-rippled tussock grass, stretching away to the encircling mountain ridges. Amongst the tussocks is a distant patch of brighter green. This is Ngamatea.

Ngamatea was first farmed in 1875 by one John Studholme, who gave it up in 1906. The property then went through several hands and a lot of money. In the early 1930s the farm was taken over by Lawrence Roberts, a dry, quiet Scotsman and a man of infinite patience, endurance and sagacity; all of which were needed in full measure.

Tussock grass has little nutritional value. It will support one wether (castrated male sheep) to three acres, but not breeding ewes. The prosperity of Ngamatea was based on the wool from a huge flock of Merino wethers who ranged semi-wild over miles of tussock and mountain. Every year these sheep had to be mustered for the shearing. The shepherds would set out with horses and the famous 'Huntaway' dogs. All supplies had to be carried on a train of pack-horses. Men and animals would live rough for days at a time as they scoured the wild and broken country that comprised each 'block', bringing in the scattered groups of wethers and combining them into a larger mob that would be driven into one of the huge holding paddocks nearer to the station. The men would then return to the same ground and do a 'straggle muster' to bring in anything that had escaped the earlier sweeps. It was hard and often dangerous work in fickle mountain weather that could have men and animals panting with thirst one day and freezing in a blizzard the next. Remember also that in the early days there were no refinements such as helicopters, radios, or telephones in the high country. The nearest town and doctor were (and are) forty miles to the west.

Times change. The wool-based economies of the great high-country stations faltered, and many went under. There were changes at Ngamatea too. Lawrence Roberts died, and the property was divided between his son Jack and his daughter Margaret. Margaret retained the home property, now reduced to a mere 80,000 acres.

Margaret is a remarkable woman and so it is hardly surprising that she married a remarkable man. Terry Apatu is a qualified valuer and a gifted agriculturalist. He and Margaret realized that if Ngamatea were to survive then it would have to change. They began a yearly cycle of reclaiming the tussock ground around the homestead. The wether flock and a lot of the back country was given up as being uneconomic.

Today the station sits in a green oasis of reclaimed pasture amidst the brown of the tussocks. The scale of the operation still blows the mind. There are 33,000 breeding ewes. These are Romney x Borrula which produce good-quality wool and a good lamb carcase.

There are 2,200 Angus x Hereford cows whose progeny all go to Japan, where they still understand what good beef ought to be. There are also 2,000 heifers and 350 red deer hinds (a new venture). The covered wool shed and handling pens stand over three-quarters of an acre. There are stands for eighteen shearers, and the annual wool output is 250,000 kilograms. On the day I was there they had 2,600 lambs drawn ready for the meat-plant lorries. The farm is so laid out that it can be worked with only five shepherds.

From their new hilltop homestead the Apatus can look out across this extraordinarily beautiful place and know that everything they can see is theirs. It is theirs in a very special sense; Margaret is the daughter of the Scottish pioneer who carved a farm out of a wilderness, and Terry is a descendant of Airini, the Maori chieftainess whose tribe leased the land for farming in the first place. I told you that Ngamatea was a Romance.

# Chapter Nine

# THAT DROTTED POND

A SMALL BURN runs along the bottom of my farm. Beside it there is a flat expanse of ground which grows good rushes but not much else. Only the hardiest of hill-bred ewes ever took their lambs down there to feed, and it appeared to be a natural breeding ground for the damaging and potentially lethal liver fluke. Every winter the little burn gets overexcited in the heavy rains and bursts its banks. The little marsh becomes a lake. All in all it seemed a very good place to fence off and dig a pond in.

A year ago I consulted my friend George. George is master of various huge pieces of yellow machinery with which he digs holes. George sucked his teeth and mentioned a telephone number as the probable cost of digging a fairly small pond, whereupon I did my own bit of tooth sucking and a lot of head shaking. We came to a compromise. He would 'put the Drott in' for forty-eight working hours, and we would see what was what at the end of that time.

The Drott and its keeper duly arrived, and for two days it snarled and grunted away in the marsh. On the third morning it sank up to the top of its tracks and lay there silent and sulking. I have somewhere a photograph of myself posing on the stricken hulk in the manner of the Sahib with his foot on a recently deceased tiger.

There the matter (and the Drott) rested. I went to the USA for two weeks. In the meantime some other machine was brought in, the Drott was rescued and the forty-eight hours completed. On my return I hurried down to see the pond. At the top of the bank I paused in astonishment: pond be blowed: this was a lake, complete with two artistic little islands. Already a spring-fed trickle of water was collecting in part of the excavation. George was justly proud of what he had accomplished.

All through the hot dry summer of 1989 I gloated at the prospect of what the winter rains and snow would bring me: a sheet of water on which wild duck would collect and by which waders would nest in the spring. The north-eastern winter of 1989–90 was one of the driest in living memory. There was little rain and less snow. The burn stayed demurely at the bottom of its channel and the lake is not. The best it has managed so far is a series of lagoons.

Patience is a great thing when dealing with nature. Grass and reeds are quietly growing along the raw scars of the banks. We have planted trees round about. The local mallard are starting to visit. An oyster catcher flew off the bank as I was walking round the other day, and the pond has its first tenants. A pair of moorhens have taken up residence and have reared a solitary chick that looks like a black bumble bee swimming about. New life is coming to the new pond. All that is needed now is some proper rain and yet more patience.


A stock farmer has to like his stock (no one would put up with the hours and aggravation otherwise), but he cannot afford to be sentimental about them. I rear my lambs so that they can eventually be killed and eaten, but I flatter myself that I am a good stockman. I take great pride in giving my sheep proper care and attention with the minimum stress involved. This is not sentiment, it is sound business practice. A comfortable and contented animal is a potentially profitable animal. I am not squeamish about the killing of animals, but I am concerned that when the end comes it should be quick and humane. For this reason I prefer that, whenever possible, my lambs go direct from the farm to the slaughter house, to be killed within a short time of their arrival.

At the moment there are certain safeguards in Britain about the feeding, resting and watering of animals in transit. These safeguards stop at the Channel. As I understand it these rules may not even apply in Britain after 1992; this would be disastrous, and I do not think that we can allow it to happen.*

* At the time of writing, hard discussions are still going on, during which the UK authorities are trying to ensure that EC regulations are 'upped' to the level of British ones.

# Chapter Ten

# THE MARKET ON THE SMOOTHFIELD

As a Primary Producer in the food chain I am accustomed to seeing my lambs for the last time in the sale ring at the local auction mart. The auctioneer's hammer falls, and they are no longer mine. They are off on a journey which ends on your Sunday luncheon table. I thought that it was time that I looked at another link in the chain.

The original market on the 'Smoothfield' was for livestock, which was driven there from all over the country to fill the ample belly of the growing City of London. The market operates under charter, and if you wanted to close it you would need an Act of Parliament. Smithfield Market is a famous place and yet I suspect that very few outsiders ever see it.

Nick Wykes is a senior man in the Union International Company, whose meat interests span the world. He had kindly agreed to be my 'minder' for my Smithfield visit. We met outside the market at 0600 hours on a cold spring morning. The present market building dates from 1868. It is a long, airy, nave-like building; the high, domed roof supported by a remarkable tracery of Victorian iron work: a cathedral dedicated to Protein and a listed building to boot. Extensive refurbishment of the market is going to be necessary to keep in line with EC requirements. The reconciliation of Ancient and Modern is going to mean telephone-number expenditure.* (*See footnote opposite.*)

The market opens at midnight, when the lorries start arriving from the abattoirs. The market handling is all manual. The carcases are brought to the back of the lorry by the 'Puller Back' and placed on the barrow of the 'Pitcher'. He wheels them to the stall of the appropriate Tenant, where the Tenant's 'cutters' take over. No meat may be removed from the market before 0500 hours. It can then only be barrowed to the buyer's lorry by a licensed 'Bummaree'. You might think that in the age of mechanical handling and fork-lift trucks all this manual work would be otiose. This is a rather delicate matter that you would have to discuss with the TGWU. No one knows the origin of the word Bummaree, but the Queen Mother is an honorary one (No. 001). which makes her the only member of the Royal Family to belong to a trade union.

Our first visit was to Derek Berry who is a pillar of Weddell, Swift: one of the largest market tenants. He was our guide for the morning. Both sides of the long central aisle are taken up by the tenants' stalls, with their wares displayed to catch the buyer's eye. There are lines of prime lamb (30,000 a week go through the market at times), and great sides of beef. There are salamis, cheeses, pies, hams, cooked meats, smoked meats, gulls' eggs, trays of quail: if it walked or flew and can be eaten, then you will find it at Smithfield.

It is necessary to be quick-witted and nimble-footed as you walk round the market. Once a heavily laden market barrow is in motion it stops for nobody. It is also quickly obvious that all the market men are in for the Cheerful Cockney Character of the Month Award (Expletives Deleted). The banter is sharp, pithy, and will probably not come up to EC Hygiene Standards.

There have been five generations of the Andrade family as Smithfield tenants. They are the only ones who have been on the same stall in the building since it opened. There are currently seven members of the family in the firm. The Andrades are one of the very few firms who still sell mutton. I would rather eat mutton than lamb any day. Philip Andrade said that most of their trade is with the ethnic groups. The Andrades are

* The future of Smithfield Market is uncertain. The cost of bringing the market up to EC standards would be enormous; the wrangle continues at the time of writing.

also big goat specialists: everything from rabbit-sized kids to big old billies. Such is the demand that they sometimes have difficulty meeting it.

We were then taken under the wing of John Brewster OBE, Managing Director of Gee and Webb and Chairman of the Tenants' Association; one of the fastest walkers I have ever tried to keep up with. We stopped at several tenants' stalls to talk about beef. It was a morning of BSE hysteria and massed TV camera teams. Beef was just not shifting, and if the Ministry of Agriculture was not suffering from a collective burning ear, then it should have been.

It was time for breakfast in the Fox and Anchor. The Smithfield public houses open at 0500 hours for the greater good of humanity. The two ladies at the next table were into their second bottle of champagne. We settled for tea and the 'Market Breakfast'. This is a standard order and consists of: two eggs, two large sausages, two fried slices, two rashers, two slices of black pudding (large), baked beans and tomatoes; sets a chap up for a bit, that does.

# Chapter Eleven

# CHARLEY, MATT AND WILLY MEET PEAT

THERE IS SOMETHING special about a peat fire. It is a warm and fragrant pleasure that very few people have experienced in these days of central over-heating. At one time peat was the most readily available fuel for remote hill farms. Peat also has the enviable quality of warming you twice: when you burn it and when you dig it; believe me, especially when you dig it.

Matt Little is one of the old school of Herds (shepherds). The Littles have lived in the Border hills for ever, and were one of the famous 'Riding Families' in the old dark days of cross-border raiding. For Matt, the hills and the sheep and his dogs are his life. He herds 2,000 sheep, and is one of the few men who still uses a horse instead of the almost ubiquitous motor bicycle. He is also one of the very few who seeks his winter fuel in the traditional way.

It was a fine June morning when Charley Dagg (another old Border name) and I met at Matt's house to 'gan to the peats'. It is three or more miles of low-ratio-geared bump and jolt out to the peat haggs, high on the hill above the ruined steading of Broadstruther. Peats must have been cut from these haggs for as long as men have lived in and farmed this wild place. Matt has been working away at the same hagg for twenty years.

Now is the time to meet the tools. The 'hayknife' is a heart-shaped blade with a short steel shank and a wide two-handed wooden T piece. These were used for cutting slices of hay from the stack in the days before bales. Now they slice through the tough heather sod that covers the peat. A parallel line is cut about one foot in from the vertical face of the old digging, then another one a foot beyond that. The long sod strip is then cut across into rectangular pieces.

The 'flouter' also has a heart-shaped blade, but with a five-foot shaft and a massive T piece. The blade has to be pushed to cut under the sods, which are then prised off. You soon learn why this tool has been nick-named the 'Man Killer'.

Some vigorous work with the flouter clears a face of brown, naked peat. The run is about two feet deep at the face, two feet wide at the top and as long as you care to make it. This is a good moment to pause, mop the brow and look about. We are about 2,000 feet up, and the great hills roll away in every direction, the dark heather contrasting with the grey bents and the bright green of the newly springing bracken. The white tufts of bog cotton sway in the welcome breeze. The only sounds are the song of the larks and the occasional blare of a ewe calling her lamb. But we are here to work.

The peats are cut out with a 'casting spade', another heart-shaped blade, but with one side turned up at a right angle to shape the sod. The cutter stands on top of the bared face, and, with both hands of the T handle, pushes the spade down into the peat to the bottom of the cut; he lifts the spade a touch, pulls back on the handle to break off the bottom, and twists out the lozenge of peat: a neat brown slice like a piece of chocolate fudge cake. The slice of peat is about eighteen inches long, by six inches wide, by four inches deep. A work rhythm soon develops: push, slice, twist; push, slice, twist. With bent back, knotted forearms and shoulders, last night's beer is soon on the run.

The man at the bottom of the hagg picks up the cut peat with a four-pronged fork and swings it up to the third man, who lays the slices out in neat rows. By lunch time there is a good showing of brown slices laid out on the heather. We sit with our backs against the Land-Rover and open our bait bags. The crack (talk) is of sheep and dogs and men; of perilous days on the hills in blizzards; of hunting the wild hill foxes.

In the afternoon we open up another face, and the rhythmic work begins again. In the old days they reckoned that a house needed a cartload of peats for every week of the year to keep the home-fire burning. I am here to tell you that a man who dug fifty-two cartloads of peats would not be worrying about his waistline. As we dig we come upon the preserved roots of birch bushes, reminders that these bare hills were once covered with birch, rowan and scrub oak.

We drain our thermos flasks at the end of the day with a feeling of satisfaction. There is a brown carpet of cut peats laid around the digging. After about two weeks they will be 'fitted', propped up in an inverted V. After two or three weeks more of sun and wind they will be built up into a cone-shaped stack called a 'rickle'. By the end of the summer the little shed behind Matt's house will be full of brick-hard blocks. There will be blue flames in the winter grate, and the sweet smell of burning peat will scent the air as it has done for hundreds of years.

# Chapter Twelve

# OF BACK ENDS, BOCHE AND BUREAUCRATS

IN OCTOBER THE view from here is congested with sheep. The back end (autumn) is the busiest time in the flockmaster's year. There is a positive orgy of matters ovine. There is jagging (injecting), dosing, dipping, feeting (pedicure) and cowing. Cowing is a Northumbrian word for the removal of the soiled wool from a sheep's nether regions. One day, whilst I was performing this rather esoteric task, I chanced to look up and there was the old man leaning on the gate. It does not matter which old man. It is quite impossible to do anything with sheep in Northumberland but an old man will come and lean on the gate and offer you the fruits of a lifetime's experience.

The old man said that he doubted I was cowing sheep (please note that 'doubt' in the north means the direct opposite to doubt in the south). I straightened up and wiped my fingers on my trousers, which is what trousers are for. How, I asked, did you spell 'cowing'? He mulled this over, and at last said that he did not ken; it was for saying, not for spelling. This may well be the first time that the word has appeared in print. I may not know how to spell it, but I do know not to use my fingers to whistle through after doing it.

To West Germany; for my first-ever visit. My feelings towards the Germans are coloured by the fact that I have never liked any of the ones that I have met. There is also the fact that they have already caused two large wars this century. My first impression of the place was favourable. The North German plain is flat and dreary, but obviously well farmed. How neat and clean everything is: everything gleams with paint and polish. Every street, pavement and lawn is spot- and speckless. There is no graffiti and the loos do not smell. After a while I began to find this very neatness rather depressing; there is a ruthlessness about such conformity. There did not look to be much room for eccentricity in Germany.

My German is minimal, so personal investigation of the German psyche was out of the question. I consulted an Englishman who has lived and worked in Germany for many years. He divided the Germans into four 'age' categories. First came the old Nazis whose only regret was that they lost. Many people in the age group forty to fifty had a genuine guilt about the war. Those in their thirties felt that if Auschwitz and Treblinka ever happened at all, they were the momentary aberration of one madman and had nothing to do with the German people. The Young and Green regret nothing, and have all their grandfathers' arrogance. My friend regards the Greens as the new Fascists, and thinks that Germany should have been kept divided at all costs. It sounds sensible to me.


By now foxhunting is in full swing throughout Britain. I love the autumn hunting, which tends to happen in the early mornings, with a select band of hardy followers. The Border Hills in October can be a place of extraordinary beauty, with a nip of frost in the early mornings, then sunlit days which bring out all the changing colours of the heather and the bracken. The air is so hard and sharp that it seems to ream out the lungs. From the high tops you can see mile upon mile of hills rolling away into the blue distance.

Every view is better if it includes a pack of hounds. I can sit on a rock high on a hill and watch hounds spread out on the opposite face, their busy noses searching for a hint of overnight fox drag. There is a high-pitched whimper, then another, then old Statesman's bass roar: 'Fox! Fox!' The whole pack swings together on the line, and the cry swells and swells as more hounds join in. It is forty years since that fierce sound first made my back hairs tingle. I still find it just as thrilling.

Rural life is a fertile breeding ground for Committees: Leek Show, Agricultural Show, Village Hall, Hunt, Hunt Supporters . . .; the list seems to be endless. You may wonder what is the major divisive social factor that plagues the smooth running of these committees. I will tell you: it is Tea versus Dinner.

The rural 5 o'clock tea is no mean and petty thing of Earl Grey and cucumber sandwiches; it is a massive stewing, frying and baking endurance test. Those who partake of it come to a 6.30 committee meeting replete and rumbling of tummy. They are then in suitable fettle to alternate pints of beer and points of order until the little hours of the morning. In the opposing corner, pinch-faced and acidulous with hunger, sits the dinner-at-eight brigade, desperate to get the meeting done for before the soufflé is.

The outcome will depend on the Chairman. The Colonel was the best I have known; with lowering brows and bristling moustache he would take the meeting along at a good hand-canter, scattering the opposition. At exactly five minutes to eight he would blow his nose and say:

'Anyotherbusiness?no?goodthenIdeclarethismeetingclosed.'
He would have the minute book under his arm and be out of the door before you could say 'point of order Brother Chair'. Democracy is a good thing, but must never interfere with dinner.

Chapter Thirteen

# A WILD LIFE IN YORKSHIRE

W<small>HAT IS A</small> FWAG? Farming and Wildlife Advisory Groups came into being in the early '70s when there was perceived to be increasing conflict between the pressures of modern farming techniques and the preservation of wildlife interests. There are sixty-five FWAGSs organized on a County basis. Each has a committee comprised of landowners, farmers and representatives of such bodies as ADAS, local Wildlife Trusts, National Parks and County Councils. Most groups now employ full-time Farm Conservation Advisers. The bulk of the funding comes from farmers and landowners.

The Derwent Foxhounds hunt a beautiful piece of North Yorkshire between Pickering and Scarborough. The Hunt recently launched a new award in conjunction with FWAG for farmers within the hunt country. The aim was to promote 'the successful integration of wildlife and landscape conservation objectives, including the maintenance and management of existing habitats and the creation of new ones, within the framework of a commercial farm'. The first prize was £250, donated by Subaru (UK) Ltd.

A competition needs judges and an organizer. The organizer was that remarkable country lady Mrs Elsie Chafer. The judges were Richard Howard-Vyse, Vice-Chairman of North Yorkshire FWAG, the Farm Conservation Adviser – Philip Lyth – and myself. Four farms had been entered for the contest, which meant a long day ahead, so we wasted no time.

Farm No. 1 was a dairy and arable farm that lay in a small dale. One side of the dale was bushes and old pasture. This had been fenced off from the cattle to protect the rare flowers that exist on the bank. The other side of the dale was fifty acres of somewhat neglected broad-leaved woodland. The hard-working young couple who own the farm started an enthusiastic system of woodland management when they took over the property. The trees were being thinned and brashed, the loppings being laid in piles to make cover for wildlife. As the timber matures, the trees will be felled and allowed to regenerate on the old coppicing system. It was in this wood that I saw my first fly orchid and bird's-nest orchid. Rare flowers are one of the glories of this dale, which is why I have not identified it. Members of the Great British Public go and dig up these orchids. (They also apparently feel that 'access' includes the right to try to cut down trees for a bit of fire-wood.)

The farm had two well-preserved dew ponds. Dew ponds are man-made, and are sited so as to catch the run-off of surface water; nothing to do with dew as I had always thought. It seems that the name comes from the great Mr Dew who made ponds for George III.

The next two farms were also in the dales. Both had embarked on ambitious schemes of planting areas of mixed woodland and digging ponds, but in both cases the judges felt that more time was needed before proper assessments could be made. At least some positive steps had been taken to enhance the landscape and to encourage wildlife; these things take time.

Our last farm was deep in the flat lands of the Vale of Pickering. George has farmed there since 1936. A stack-yard pond is a rare sight these days. This one was thick with yellow flags and bulrushes. An old green lane still ran through the middle of the farm. The landlord had once suggested that it should be ripped out in the interests of efficiency, but George reckoned that he could be just as efficient by keeping the lane and its wild flowers. The hedges were neatly trimmed at the sides but allowed to grow upwards giving good shelter for birds and stock.

Ten little copses had been planted in field corners. A smart-looking field of oats had a strip of kale planted right round it to give good game covert. A big old pasture ran down one side of the farm. The mediaeval field strips could still be seen.

Many of these old pastures with their varied herbage were famous 'feeding grounds' for stock; 'were' because thousands of acres have been ripped out to grow poor corn. It should be remembered that there was strong political encouragement to do this. Many farmers have come to regret their impetuosity.

George's delight in his farm and its wildlife was obvious. He talked of the wonderful birdsong in the mornings and the two breeds of fox cubs. Yet everything he had done was 'within the framework of a commercial farm'.

All the farmers we met were impressive in their enthusiasm for what they were trying to do, and their pride in what had been achieved. It would have been nice to give them all a prize, but there was only one: we all felt that it had to go to George.

Chapter Fourteen

# OF HILLS, HAM SANDWICHES AND PARATROOPERS

A CUP OF COFFEE with Ian and Les seemed a good way to start a walk. Father and son farm far up the Coquet Valley. The remote valley farms have no main services. All electricity is supplied by a diesel generator. You do not get power cuts with a 'genny', but you have to think before you press a switch. To be able to turn the electric kettle on, you have to turn something else off. But, as Les says, it is better than paraffin lamps, and you learn to live with the constraints. Just above the farm is the old School House. Many generations of farm children would have trudged there from isolated steadings. Some of them would have walked miles in their bare feet. The building is full of hay now. The old road from the farm is slung across the hillside like a loose strap. It was a close, airless morning, and the track gets steeper all the time; but I was determined not to stop until I reached the crest of the first ridge. Over the ridge is a secret valley with a small river dashing along the bottom. The day was so still that I could hear the running water hundreds of feet below.

On the other side of the valley is a small farm that has disappeared under conifers. The house is still there, in a sheltered corner of the hill and on the river bank. This property is for sale and has recently been advertised in the glossy magazines as a 'private retreat'. There is no estate agent's hyperbole in the description of the house as 'a beautifully isolated cottage'. The advertisement does not touch on the fact that the vehicular access is somewhat limited; as it might be to a 4 × 4 tractor. In the winter snows the retreat would be very private indeed.

On the ridge above the cottage my track joins a main road. This is the famous Clennell Street, which used to be one of the main trunk routes between England and Scotland. I was the only traffic on it, but before you get too excited about leaping into your car and having a burn up, let me advise you that the road is totally Porsche-proof.

The little valley broadened out in front of me. At the top of it lies one of the most remote farms in England. A plume of smoke rose from the chimney. At one time there were five shepherds employed on this farm. Now a big part of it has also gone to conifers. One man and his family herd what is left. A red beetle crawling along the valley side enlarged into the post van. There is a stone track to the farm. It must be four miles and several gates to a tarmac road, then another fifteen curly miles to the nearest shop.

After crossing the farm road it is another two miles of a hike to the top of the main ridge; a long, steady, uphill pull. Then through a gate and you are in Scotland, with the dramatic views of the Bowmont valley below and the fat lowlands of the River Tweed in the distance. Many an English reiver must have halted at this spot and licked his lips at the prospect of all those lovely, juicy Scottish sheep and cattle waiting to be lifted.

The Windy Gyle is well named, but, for once, there was hardly a breath of wind on top of this great hill. I found a comfortable stone, and with my bum in England and my feet in Scotland opened my bait bag: ham sandwiches with plenty of mustard and a flask of strong tea; what could be better? The view from the Gyle on a clear day is amazing, but it was hazy, and anyway, the view was suddenly full of Belgian paratroopers. They seemed somewhat confused by the sight of a fat man in huge boots eating ham sandwiches. But they were very polite. 'Goot mornink,' said the Lieutenant. 'Bonjour, monsieur: ça va?' said I. This seemed to confuse them even more; not too many French speakers on the Windy Gyle I suppose.

The Belgians and I set off for the valley road at the same time but in different directions. I am not a competitive person, but it just seemed a good idea (if not a patriotic duty) to get to the valley road first. It was downhill all the way now, but walking downhill can be a different sort of hard work: tones up the thigh muscles no end. That is what they say about exercising horses: uphill for wind; downhill for muscle.

The road was empty when I reached it. I saw no one but sheep as I plodded along beside the rushing Coquet. My muscles said that 12.4 miles on the pedometer called for a pint at the Rose and Thistle; it is no good having one pint without the other. There was still no sign of the Belgians, so I declared a peace dividend of a third pint and went home.

Chapter Fifteen

# 'ISTHA GANNIN' T'SHOW LIKE?'

'HEY OOP, YOUNG MAN! Watch thee back!' The crowd parts swiftly as the Longhorn Bulls file aldermanically out of their show ring. Their magnificent horns command respect. 'Bye I wouldn't fancy being pushed by one of them, wor lass.' Longhorns are an ancient breed, handsome, red-and-white mottled beasts, whose ancestors were once much in demand as draught oxen and suppliers of meat. The breed was endangered but is now undergoing a revival.

A well-modulated tannoy commands the presence of the Ridden Hunter Classes in the Main Ring. There are frantic last-minute polishings in the collecting ring to horses and tack already gleaming. A quick duster is run over the mirror-like perfection of a rider's boots, whilst he nervously adjusts the bowler hat. There must be no slight imperfections to catch the eagle eye of the Judge. But what of the Judge? A flustered huddle of dark-suited and bowler-hatted officials suggests that a problem has arisen. The Eminent Irish Judge is apparently still in Ireland, lost in some misty Celtic time warp.

The clump of heavy hooves, the jingle of harness and the grinding of iron-shod wheels makes the crowd draw respectfully to the sides of the road. It is Bankside Charley, a magnificent Shire horse, pulling Mr Parker's Yorkshire Wool Wagon. Shire horses are the gentle giants of the draught horse world. They were the only motive power on the farm of my Cornish childhood. It is good that enthusiasts have kept the breed going through the flood of post-war mechanization. Geoff Swann, who drives the wagon, has worked with heavy horses all his life. He thinks that the wagon itself is over a hundred years old: 'That's t'bloody driver, more like,' says an anonymous voice from the crowd.

Two mounted policemen keep the entrance to the collecting ring clear. A small boy stares up at these amazing beings: 'Is your horse fifteen feet?' he asks one of the policemen. 'Nay, lad, he's nobbut sixteen hands.'

This is the Great Yorkshire Show. Summer in Britain is the time for Agricultural Shows. Agricultural shows vary greatly in size and intensity. At one end of the scale is my favourite local show. This takes place at a windswept crossroads high in the Border Hills. There may be a couple of score of sheep on display. A few foxhounds and terriers will be shown in the rough-cut grass ring. The real reason for this show is that the site boasts a spring whose water is unusually pure and beneficial in character. By mixing this water judiciously with whisky, an elixir is formed such as may banish all foul thoughts, and lead to singing and dancing.

The Great Yorkshire makes no such claim for the water which it uses at the rate of 15,000 gallons per hour. However it does aim to provide a chance for all sorts and conditions of people to come together, enjoy themselves and forget their troubles for a day, or three. This is the Jam on the Bread. Bread is what all agricultural shows are basically about.

When the Yorkshire Agricultural Society held its first show in 1838, its objectives were 'the improvement of agriculture and associated industries and the breeding of livestock; the demonstration of improved methods ... and the encouragement of agricultural education and research'. These aims still hold good. Farmers come to see and argue about best breeds of livestock. They still come to scratch their heads at new advances in farm machinery. They queue to take glasses of gin off jovial-for-the-occasion bank managers. They may even listen, with polite scepticism, to the verbal bromides from the Politician of the Day ('My dog's got more sense than yon booger').

Agriculture is still the biggest single industry in Britain. The shows are the industry's display cases. In a country that is now ninety-five per cent urban it is important to remember that man does not live by supermarkets alone. The food and drink on the shelves has to be produced by farmers. Agricultural shows allow the public to see the primary sources of their ham sandwich or their meat pie, and to rub shoulders with those who produce them ('OW! he trod on my foot, Albert'). The Great Yorkshire Show is a good example of the Thoroughly Modern and Successful Show.

At one time it was the custom for these shows to move round the county. The increase in size and logistical problems has forced them to become established on permanent showgrounds. These days it is quite possible that the daily attendance figure at a major show will be in the 30,000–40,000 range. These people will want to park their cars and walk about with the minimum interference from good old British mud. They will want a continuous selection of entertainments to gawp at. They will want to shop for everything from a pair of green wellies to an air-conditioned, computer-bedecked combine harvester.

The visitors will require varying degrees of browsing and sluicing. As sure as night follows day they will then need a multiplicity of efficient cloacal arrangements. There will be a Police, Fire and Ambulance presence, and a beehive of harassed, but efficient, Administrative Staff. All this means permanent buildings and permanent walkways around all of which a city of tents, marquees and caravans will mushroom for the duration of the show. There has to be proper accommodation for some 2,000 assorted animals and their keepers, and arrangements for feeding, watering and waste disposal. It costs somewhere in the region of £800,000 (1990) to put on a major show.

In the early years the Show moved from town to town throughout Yorkshire, that is the old and rightful Yorkshire of the Three Ridings. In 1950 the Society purchased land outside Harrogate and established a permanent site for what had become popularly known as the 'Great' Yorkshire Show. The name and the site have maintained until the present. The showground itself covers one hundred acres, with 150 acres of car parks, which can cope with 45,000 cars.

The setting is now in suburbia, which makes access to the showground a nightmare of creeping traffic locks. Trouble-free access to the present site is really only possible if arrival is planned before both the daily commercial Harrogate traffic and the Show traffic combine in a steamy embrace.

This early arrival may present the problem of finding some breakfast. The public catering has not yet rubbed the sleep from its eyes, but there may well be bacon and coffee smells coming from the places that cater for rarefied people like judges, stewards and others of high degree. A suit, a moustache and an imposing front can sometimes gain entry to such places for unqualified, but hungry, persons. This is not a proper course of action.

A man refreshed (having wiped the recent egg from his moustache) may then set out to wander the, as yet, uncrowded showground. It is a good time to visit the trade stands. Here may be seen the latest designs in equipment for the stress-free handling of livestock. A good handling system is more expensive than the tangle of ramshackle hurdles and pieces of rusty corrugated iron that many farmers still justify on the grounds of economy. Things like hernias, slipped discs, muddles, general bad temper and blood poisoning from the rusty iron are not taken into account.

Wander on down the line of stands: designer knitwear – universal drills – jaunty hats; any use to any of you? Now here is a place to keep your wife away from. There are goodies to whet the appetite and seriously damage the chequebook.

Johnny Mead was once a dashing Horse Gunner and rider of amateur steeplechases. He developed a skill in working wood, and now makes high-class fitted kitchens, tantalizingly on show here. Mr Major will be comforted to hear that his recession is biting, and that it is enterprising businesses like John Mead Country Kitchens that are bearing the teeth marks.

The well-set bowler hat and well-built suit contain Michael Abrahams. Mr Abrahams is dedicated to renewing interest in the breed of Shorthorn Cattle. These attractive mottled beasts were once widespread, but have become eclipsed in recent years by the fashion for larger Continental breeds; farmers being as fashion conscious as any Harrogate Housewife. Mr Abraham's young bull has just taken a Reserve, and his eyes shine with revivalist fervour as he expounds on the great future for the Improved Shorthorn.

A wander through the cattle lines presents a great variety of breeds: the South Devons of my youth – but now without their horns – Lincoln Reds, Aberdeen Angus and Herefords, from which breeds come the best of British Beef. There are British Charollais, huge and white, and the hardy, shaggy Galloways. The cattle sheds are a frenzy of polishing, shampooing and crimping, the atmosphere heavy with pre-show tension and hot methane. The end of one of the cattle sheds is covered in creeper. Four wagtail chicks have somehow been dislodged from their nest, and are standing on the pavement demanding food. The mother continues to fly in to fill the gaping beaks, seemingly paying no attention to the stream of passing people.

There are always displays of skill at agricultural shows. W. B. Tegetmeier is the only thatcher in the north-east of England. He works from Lincolnshire to Scotland. For the duration of the show he is demonstrating his skill by thatching a small structure that might come in useful as a 'netty' (outside privy). He uses mainly rye or wheat straw. It takes three to four tons to thatch a small cottage, and thereby hangs a problem. Thatching straw has to be of a certain type and a certain length. It has to be cut with a binder and threshed in the old-fashioned way. Few farmers can produce this straw now, and scarcity accounts for prices of £250–£350 per ton. It is noteworthy that more building firms are showing an interest in thatch, with its marvellous insulating qualities, for new houses. Mr Tegetmeier has a year's work on his books; a happy man who loves what he does.

More stalls: baskets, sticks, buns, guns, knives: a good chance to buy a new knife for gralloching, and a folding saw for sawing. A smart line in patter to sell kitchen knives: '. . . buy a knife and I throw in another for free. You can give it to a friend or use it on your mother-in-law . . .'

Ian and Jean Healey run the Sportingman's Bookshop. They spend the summer travelling from show to show with their caravan and stall of books. Here you can buy all and every book to do with the countryside and country pursuits: 'Hunting: an Introductory Guide'; 'A Backwoodsman's Year'; 'Shooting and Stalking'; 'Farmer's Ordinary'; 'Outside Days': these are the sort of books that keep the till ringing: not a Bodice Ripper in sight.

All northern shows have a display of 'dressed sticks'. A good stick is as much part of a shepherd's daily life as are his boots. The show sticks are the result of hours of skill and patience, their curved horn heads amazingly carved: a fox creeps up on an unsuspecting rabbit; a collie confronts a stamping Swaledale ewe. The detail is minute.

As the day goes on both the crowd and the heat start to increase: time for a little something. A corner of the showground is devoted to the shining, mechanical behemoths of the farm machinery section. This is a good place to seek a glass of gin and some information. The machinery business is a good barometer of the state of farming: it 'lives off the farmer's back'.

John Gill and Sons is a family company that has been exhibiting at the Great Yorkshire since 1873, which makes it the longest serving exhibitor. Malcolm Gill, the Sales Director, is gloomy about the state of agriculture and its allied trades. Things are not good. Farmers are pulling their belts up yet another notch. Several old-established machinery businesses have recently gone into liquidation. Turnover may rise with inflation but profit margins are squeezed ever tighter.

But people come to the Great Yorkshire to forget their troubles for the day. There is always entertainment at agricultural shows, with several different things happening at the same time in the various rings and display areas. The ceaseless thumping of the inevitable military band clashes with the braying of the tannoy announcements, and the increasingly querulous requests for 'Major Galbraith to come to the Secretary's Office': what can the good Major be up to?

Should you find that the seemingly endless Ridden Hunter classes begin to pall a bit, then why not seek out the J. C. B. Dancing Diggers; an intricate display of mechanical ballet by those large machines that are usually digging up the road when you are late for work. There will be show jumping: OOH! for each successful levitation and AAAH! as the triple bars are turned into spillikins.

Sheep-shearing displays always attract a crowd. How does

that lissom, half-naked man manoeuvre a 150-lb sheep with one hand and a knee, whilst removing its jacket in what seems like one continuous movement of the clipper? If you knew the answer to that then you too could clip 300 sheep a day and be slim and well-paid.

There will certainly be a parade by a local pack of fox-hounds. This is always a brave sight, greeted with enthusiasm; it is a major test of nerves for the huntsman, however, especially if his over-fresh horse, resenting the interruption of its summer holiday, starts to buck in the ring; I know.

By midday the air is heavy with the smell of vinegar, onions, chips and greasy burgers: luncheon is in the offing. The best luncheon at the Great Yorkshire is produced at the Hound Show by Mr Romford, the prince of peripatetic caterers. You have to become a Vice President to avail yourself of the privilege of sampling his rare roast beef and salmon *en croûte*, but that is a small price to pay. The inevitable glass of port that follows helps to put agricultural shows in perspective.

Agricultural shows are a mirror of the countryside. The shows are still show-cases for British agriculture, and a proud demonstration of its excellence. This is doubly important in a time of changing attitudes. Great Britain is now an urban country. Urban Man no longer sees the countryside as a place of work and food production. He is coming increasingly to regard it as a place for recreation. Agricultural shows bring Town and Country together. This mixing may just remind Urban Man that people do live and work in the countryside. It may also remind a farmer that there are people out there beyond the farm gate, and that they are his eventual customers. The Great Yorkshire Show does a good job: I raise my glass of port to its continued good health.

Chapter Sixteen

# LES SCOOTS

THE MAJOR AND I were sitting on a crag in the late
August sunshine. Far below us the hounds were doing not
very much in a huge bracken bed. Our pipes were drawing
nicely, and we were both at peace with the world.

'Have Les Scoots gone?'

A spasm that might have been pain appeared momentarily
on the Major's face. 'Midnight last night, thank God,' he
said.

The Major is a kindly and public-spirited man. As well as
being a hard-working and successful farmer, he is also the local
Master of Foxhounds, Chairman of this, President of that and
Head Honcho of just about any local organization that you
may care to mention, including the local Scouts. He had just
hosted an international gathering of more than 2,000 Scouts
on his land. This had passed off well, except for excessive
wear and tear on the nerves of his gamekeeper. This unfortunate man had been so overcome at the thought of 2,000
Scouts amongst his pheasants that he had fled to Wester Ross
for the duration of their stay. Otherwise all would have been
peace and harmony, but for the Germans and the French. They
had steadfastly refused to fraternize, not only with their scouting brothers from across the world, but also with each other.
This meant that when happy international coach trips were
arranged to local beauty spots, there also had to be a separate
coach for the Germans and yet another for the French. So
much for the Spirit of European Unity.

At last the Scouts folded their tents and departed. The
keeper returned rather gingerly from his exile and life returned
to normal.

Then Les Scoots arrived. There is a truly excellent little restaurant, in a small street, hard by the Cathedral of Notre Dame. Some two years ago you would have found me there, enjoying a Lucullian luncheon with my old friend M Alberique. It was during the demolition of some particularly scrumptious duck and a magnificent Volnay that Alberique broached the subject of his Scoots (French for Scouts). It seemed that he was the Commissaire of his local Scoots. He was very keen that they should voyage into England, especially to some country-side very savage. Just such a countryside, is it not, where you inhabit, My Old? There they could test their skills in the survival and the endurance, it is good?

Monsieur le Patron materialized with yet another bottle and filled my glass with all the proper ceremony. Nothing would be more easy I told M Alberique. My good friend the Major was also a Commissaire. He would be delighted to welcome Les Scoots, well sure. Well sure, the Major came up trumps. After all, he reasoned, with 2,000 Scouts another fifty Scoots would not make a lot of difference.

The trouble was that Les Scoots were different. They were a Schism. They regarded the mainstream Scout movement as decadent. They wanted a more rugged form of scouting, where the chaps used their initiative and lived off the country. They would have nothing to do with the main gathering. So as the Scouts moved out, Les Scoots moved in.

Each patrol built a separate little camp down by the river. They made ingenious stoves and ovens from holes in the ground. Their beds were made from frames of branches and rope. It soon became obvious that 'living off the country' meant making use of anything that was not nailed down and secured with at least three padlocks.

A little shrine was built by each patrol, at which morning devotions took place. *Les Aigles* built their shrine inside a large enclosure designed for the protection of young pheasants, to the consternation of the young birds and the even greater consternation of the keeper. This good man's unhappiness was compounded when he discovered that they had also dug their latrine pit in the pen. He also found out (too late) that it had been rather well concealed. Reeking at this injustice, he turned off their water supply. Relations became strained, and the Major had to mediate.

The Scoots' foraging expeditions took them far and wide. The Major got an enraged telephone call from a keen gardener in the next village, who, on looking out of his bedroom window first thing in the morning, found six Scoots asleep in the flower bed that had contained some prize blooms.

They found their way to the cricket match at Bullingham and scoffed the tea when no one was looking. They were apprehended and made to wash up, under guard. It was unfortunate that they left a generous layer of washing-up liquid in the kettle. When the ladies came to boil the kettle on the following weekend, the kitchen filled with foam. They attended the local motorbike scramble with great enthusiasm. That night all the ropes from the course were liberated.

As friends of M Alberique, my wife and I were given a tour of the encampment as honoured guests. I was particularly impressed with the culinary arrangements. The Lynx patrol had four fat pheasant poults about to go into their earthen oven. As far as I could understand it, the pheasants had just been passing by and had stopped for supper.

The Leopards had a leg of lamb on the go. I asked no more questions. Indeed with any difficult question, Les Scoots took refuge in a cloud of Gallic incomprehension. They did have an interpreter: an American scout on attachment from New York, who spoke a sort of Runyonesque patois. He, very shrewdly, made himself scarce at moments of crisis.

No one has yet discovered exactly what enormity Les Scoots perpetrated by way of a farewell to the keeper. What is known is that the sorely tried man was seen pursuing a body of them down the lane, waving a shovel and screaming ' . . . . off! . . . . off! . . . . off!' Now it seemed that they had finally done so.

The Major brooded for a moment, as though dark thoughts were passing through his mind. Then he tapped out his pipe and said quietly: 'I do not think that I ever want to hear the word Scoot again.' Ah well, *c'est la vie*.

# Chapter Seventeen

# FIRST CATCH YOUR MINK

A s Field Sports go, Mink Hunting is a baby. There were no wild mink in Britain. The present population started with escapees from mink farms, many having been 'liberated' by 'Animal Rights Activists'. No doubt these people were full of righteous intent, but the end result of their thoughtless action has been disaster for some of our indigenous wildlife. Mink are highly successful, semi-aquatic predators. They eat just about anything that moves in and around water. They are also great climbers, so no nests are safe. On my stretch of burn this spring, I had a brood of mallard and a brood of moorhens. The young ducks have gone and the whole family of moorhens has been terminated with extreme prejudice: no 'Animal Rights' for them.

The rise in the mink population coincided with, and contributed to, the decline of the otter in most parts of Britain. The Masters of Otterhounds Association took a very proper decision to cease hunting the otter in 1978. Many hunts turned their attention and their skills to dealing with the new scourge.

The West Yorkshire Mink Hounds were founded in 1980. The presiding genius is Mr Bob Auty, a planning officer with the National Park Authority. All the Hunt Staff do other jobs and look after the hounds in their spare time. Allan Jarvis, the huntsman, sells Mercedes cars for a living. Colin Bradley is a gas man. Colin Rivers works for the Water Board. Angus Munro does 'a little bit of everything'. The hunt operates mainly in Yorkshire and Lancashire, but they visit rivers further north when their services are requested. It is a firm policy that the mink hounds do not hunt any water where otters are known to be resident.

The West Yorkshire recently met at Allensford Hall, in Co Durham, to hunt a stretch of the River Derwent at the request of the riparian owners. About fifty local enthusiasts joined the visiting Yorkshiremen. The hounds were mostly foxhounds, with a few shaggy pure-bred otterhounds and some cross-breds. Terriers are important for mink hunting. There were some impressive-looking Border terriers with the length of leg to run and swim all day. There were also the only two working Sealyhams that I have ever seen: a real pair of hard nuts.

It was unfortunate that there had been a violent storm during the previous night, which had brought down a tremendous spate. Filter bed operators like to make best use of a spate, which may have helped to make the river look like strong cocoa. Conditions did not look very promising, when you consider that hounds hunt entirely by scent.

Mink-hunting dress is not terribly formal. The Hunt Staff looked very smart in yellow waistcoats and blue breeches. Everybody else wore whatever they fancied for five or six hours of walking, wading, scrambling up and down muddy banks, falling in bramble patches and forcing a boggy path through beds of head-high willow herb. Strong, tackety shoes and plus-fours are good, and a stout stick is a welcome friend when wading waist deep in a torrent. Full marks to the lady in tight skirt and high-heeled shoes who kept going all day.

Numerous sightings of mink had been reported, but it was obvious that the spate had driven them from their normal haunts. We must have walked for an hour before a hound spoke for the first time. More joined the chorus, and we had a fine sight of hounds and the game little terriers swimming the wide river. There was a cricket match in progress on the bank. The excitement attracted some of the weaker brethren in the outfield. The huntsman worked hounds up- and down stream with great perseverance, but to no avail. Hounds drew on downstream.

Even the spells of inactivity were pleasant. All the time we were walking along beautiful, wooded river-banks; the day was fine, the company pleasant, and if you got too hot then you waded the river. We passed through a steep rocky gorge:

a wild and picturesque place, which had been generously decorated with old mattresses and rusting domestic appliances by local nature lovers.

Below the gorge we came to a thick swamp of alder and willow herb. There was a burst of hound voices: there was a mink about. For the thick end of an hour, hounds and huntsman worked patiently. Hounds were able to speak here and there, but never to get the mink up and running. There was neither sight, nor scent, to be had in the chocolate flood. This was not really surprising as we had recently passed another filter bed, which had patently been making a contribution. I felt for the hardy souls who were wading about up to their chests. Although the afternoon heat was brutal, I had lost my enthusiasm for cooling off. Hounds continued to persevere down stream. I admired their tenacity, but conditions were all against them and, at about 6.00 p.m., a halt was called.

It had been my first day's mink hunting and I found it most interesting. The services of the mink hounds are in great demand. They help control a destructive little animal that should never have been a problem in this country. But let us not blame the mink for the damage it does. The fault lies with the misguided people who let it loose on our wildlife in the first place.

Chapter Eighteen

# 'WHEN I SHOWED HER THE WORKS OF MY THRESHING MACHINE' [*Trad.*]

A RECENT VISIT TO Tot and Anne Hutchinson at the
Haining Farm Park brought about a massive bout of
nostalgia. With their neighbour, Geoff Bell, they had put on a
threshing demonstration. It took me back to my Cornish
childhood. In those far-off days, before the advent of the
combine harvester (which cuts and threshes on the job, as it
were) the corn was cut with a binder pulled by real horse-
power. The straw stems, complete with head, were drawn up
into the innards of the machine, where a mechanical knotter
tied them off into sheaves, which then dropped out behind.
The sheaves were then put (manually) into stooks, like little
wigwams, so that rain would run off them and the sun and
wind could work on them. In due course they would be
carried on the wagon, pulled by two massive Shire horses, to
the stack yard. Here the sheaves would be built into ricks. All
this was done by muscle power, prongs (pitch forks) and
liberal draughts of home-made cider.

In the autumn came the ponderous threshing machine,
rumbling through the narrow lanes from farm to farm. At one
time it would have been pulled and worked by a steam engine,
but latterly the power was provided by one of the new-fangled
tractors. The purpose of the threshing was to separate the
grain from the straw. Sheaf after sheaf was fed into the grum-
bling mechanical Moloch. As the rick dwindled, there would
be cries of 'Rats! Rats!', and there would be a flurry of dogs

and boys and sticks. My first action on arriving at the Haining was to tuck the end of my trousers into my socks. Old habits die hard. The thought of a rat up my trouser leg appeals no more now than it did forty years ago. There were no vermin. The sheaves of barley used for the demonstration had only recently been cut with Geoff's binder and brought across for the occasion.

Tot bought his thresher at a farm sale for £200. It is a static machine, which had stood all its previous one hundred years in the same barn. The power was provided by Geoff's forty-year-old Ferguson tractor, one of the famous little 'Grey Fergies'. The thresher is driven by a continuous belt. The sheaf is fed head first through an opening at the top of the machine where the whirling drum strips the grain from the heads with a sinister tearing sound. Threshing drums caused many a maiming and fatal accident in the past.

The straw is pulled by the drum on to a conveyor that pushes it out at the back of the machine. The grain falls down into the bowels past a powerful winnowing fan that blows it clean of the chaff. The grain then comes out through a chute on the side and into a waiting sack. The chaff does the same thing through a separate chute. Everything is worked by a connecting series of belts, wheels and cranks. It is noisy: chugging, clanking, rattling, and the screaming whirr of the drum. The large crowd of spectators regarded the massive machine with awe and respect.

Tot's idea was to show a complete process of natural food production. The threshed barley was put into the mill (driven by another old Fergie). The mill can be set two ways. A roller will 'bruise' the grain to make it more easily digestible for animal feed. We all trooped off to see a bucket of bruised barley being fed to Nanny, the Suffolk Cross ewe, and her three lambs.

Set the mill to grind small and you get a coarse flour called 'crowdie'. You can mix this with a little water and make delicious scones. Mix it with a lot more water and there is a nourishing feed for Katie and Liz, the Tamworth pigs. Tamworths are a red-brown colour and a 'Rare Breed'. There is something particularly satisfying about the sight and sound (especially the sound) of healthy pigs tucking into their grub.

Roly Robson still works horses on his farm. He and his father used to run a mobile threshing machine. They would start in October and be on the road until the following May, all through the Tyne valley. Did he never get sick of it? 'We knew nowt else, man.' A threshing day was a communal effort. All the neighbours would rally round. The sheaves would be forked up, caught on the platform, their bands cut and the loose sheaf handed to the operator who fed the drum. The straw had to be forked away and stacked. The bags of corn (eight-, twelve-, even sixteen-stone sacks) and the chaff bags had to be tied and manhandled away. All this meant a team of seventeen to twenty men. Hard work makes hungry men. Huge meals were provided. There might be a variation from 'mutton, taties and turnip', but by tradition, afters was always a huge rice pudding. Hungry men are not too squeamish. One day a disturbed mouse jumped into the rice pudding: 'Way, wor Tom just felled it with a spoon and hoyed it oot.'

There were home-made scones for tea at the Haining, and not a mouse in sight, but the day had brought back memories for many of us. Said Roly: 'They were better days, man. We all helped each other. We worked hard, but the crack (fun) was great.'

Chapter Nineteen

# SERMONS IN STONES

THE OTHER DAY I was crossing a bit of hill which was not well known to me. It is a desolate piece of country: peat hagg, heather, and rock: lots of rock. I remember thinking that if there was money in rock, then you would get rich farming this ground; as things are it would be a job to keep the seat in the family trousers. Then I came upon the millstone, lying half-buried in the heather. It was a mystery. I presented the mystery to Tommy and Geordie, whose local knowledge is encyclopaedic. They knew the stone and another similar one further along the hill. There was also a large stone trough which was perfect in every particular except that it had one end missing. The cutter had obviously been putting the finishing touches to the end when he struck a fault, or hammered too hard, and the end fell off. It seems that men would go out to the gill, find a suitable piece of rock, and hammer and chip away until they had hewed out the required article: hard and lonely work. I could not but feel for the unfortunate chap who had chiselled and chipped to make that trough and then seen all his hard work destroyed by one careless stroke.

'Twa stanes abuin (above) a stane and a stane abuin twa – pin weel and pack weel and ye'll big (build) a guid wa''; there you are: now you know how to build a dry-stone dyke (wall).

Tom Arres of Kelso has been building stone dykes for most of his working life. He came from a long line of Herds (shepherds), but never took to the job. He took to dyking because he wanted to leave his mark on the countryside, something that will be there long after he is dead and buried. Tom is an artist, and his work can be seen all over Roxburghshire and its fringes. As a good stone dyke should stand for 100–200 years, he should have quite a memorial by the time he hands in his stone-working hammer.

I met him on an estate at the eastern end of the Cheviot Hills. He has already done several miles of dyking on this estate over the years. The neat lines of his handiwork stand out proudly on the bleak, wind-blasted landscape. He was working on the renovation of an old tumbled wall, which he reckoned would have been put up at the time of the original enclosure of the land, probably early in the last century.

Tom works with his son Mark, who started at seventeen and is now twenty-five. Did Mark never feel that he wanted to do something else? 'Aye, often,' said with a wry smile. It has to be said that dyking is hard and sometimes monotonous work, usually in the teeth of the weather. The other members of the team are Jim Young, who has been twelve years with Tom, and Grant Morrison, who was off sick that day.

This stretch of dyke was in the National Park, which meant that Tom contracts with the National Park and not the land-owner. All dykes in the National Park have the coping stones cemented on to prevent irresponsible ramblers pushing them off when they scramble over them. The dykers work a twelve-yard stretch at a time. The neat work behind them contrasted strongly with the tumbled line that ran uphill before them. The working stretch was surrounded with a tumble of stones of all sizes in the reddish colour of Cheviot granite.

Was it necessary to dismantle a wall to rebuild it? Tom shook his head. 'You never disturb another man's work if it is sound.' So how is a stone dyke constructed? 'A dyke has three sides: this side, yon side and the inside – the inside is the most important.'

Think of a gymnasium vaulting-horse: that is the approximate shape of the classic stone 'double dyke'. It should be 28 inches wide at the bottom, tapering to 14 inches at the top, below the coping stones. The standard height to the top of the coping stones is 4 feet 6 inches. The inward-sloping sides are built of big 'doubles' of different shapes and sizes. Whenever one is available, a long, heavy 'bandstone' is laid through the wall from side to side; this gives added strength. Every double has to grip the two beneath it across the join. The interior of the wall is packed with small 'hearting' stones. The wall is capped with a large 'coverband' stone, and then the 'coping' stones cap the job. The gaps between the doubles are filled with small 'pinnings'.

The dyker's main tool is a small hammer, tapered at one side of the head. Tom and Jim work opposite each other, keeping exactly level at all times. Think on a pile of plates, says Tom, if they lie level and are stacked level, they will lie till the table rots; you can push them off, but they will never fall off. From the pile of loose stones each man's expert eye is able to select the right stone for the right place, to give overlap and grip. If an exact requirement is not available, Tom turns over several stones until he finds just what he wants. A couple of taps with the hammer splits the stone, and hey presto, there is the precise stone. It all looks so easy, but everything looks easy when a skilled man is doing it. Dyking is difficult. Tom reckons that a good dyker has to be at it all day and every day. Even if he goes on holiday, he finds that he is 'awkward as anything' when he first starts back at work.

The dyke grows steadily through the morning, then comes the search for coping stones, which are selected for their looks as well as their strength; 'a dyke is like a wife; you want something worth looking at.' To me it looks a beautifully neat job, but Tom is not happy, the stones have not worked well for him: 'It's rough, it's rough: try as ye might ye canna get it any better.'

On my way down the track from the hill, I stop to open a gate in a well-set dyke. There is a stone in the dyke with 'Arres and Son – 1986' chiselled into it. Tom's handiwork webbed the hillside. 'A Sermon in Stone' does not seem to be a bad marker for a man to leave behind him.

## Chapter Twenty

# HARES, PHEASANTS AND GUNS IN SUFFOLK

THE LAST TWENTY years have produced a great surge of interest in Field Sports. There are more people seeking to take part in the traditional pastimes of Hunting, Shooting and Fishing than there have ever been. It is certainly true that the New Sportsmen bring with them money and support at a time when all Field Sports are under a political threat, but they also bring certain problems. The essence of all Field Sports is that they should be part of the natural process of culling and regeneration. Bred-and-buttered country people grow up with this delicate balance, and understand it instinctively; the New Sportsman does not have this advantage.

The problem is most acute in the shooting world. There is nothing to stop a man with a Shotgun Certificate and a Game licence joining a shoot, even though he may never have handled anything more lethal than a mobile telephone. This problem has been compounded by the growth of Corporate Entertainment. Big businesses take days' shooting, or even rent their own shoots, to which they invite favoured clients. In case you are wrinkling your brows as to how this might appear in the accounts, you might try under 'Staff Welfare', or 'Management Training'. It is unfortunate that Management Training does not include anything to do with firearms safety, or a respect for the quarry, the countryside, and those who live there.

Robin and Maggie Hare are dedicated shooting people and naturalists. The Hare family have lived and farmed in Suffolk for four generations. Robin runs an intensive 300-acre arable unit, but he is passionate about the wild life on the farm. The old broadleaved woodlands are coppiced. Hedgerows are left wild. Four ponds have been dug and stocked with fish. All straw is incorporated, and grass verges are left on all arable fields. This means butterflies and barn owls, wild flowers and partridges, and, of course, pheasants, because the shoot is the catalyst for all this preservation.

Robin is also involved with running a large commercial shoot on which 'New Guns' (those who shoot are called 'Guns') frequently appear. Some commercial shoots have a dubious reputation both for safety and sportsmanship. The Hares felt that something had to be done to promote traditional sporting values; so the Fordley Hall Country Sports Course came to be. It is an intensive two-day course for those who have the sense to admit that they are new to driven-game shooting. The course has so far been attended by solicitors, lorry drivers, surgeons, mechanics, civil servants and more. Ladies are welcome. Maggie Hare is a fine shot.

The first emphasis of the course is on safety; as Robin says: 'There can be no compromising on safety on the driven-game field. The shotgun is a lethal weapon ... people who shoot dangerously are a menace and should not be allowed to continue.' In the old days of private shoots, the host sent people home if they were dangerous. The matter becomes more ticklish if the offender is an important business client and large sums of money are involved. Such people (and their guns) have to be tactfully pointed in the right direction. The course also seeks to emphasize the fun and fellowship that goes with shooting.

The morning of the first day is taken up with lectures: Legislation, Gun Safety, Shooting's Contribution to the Environment (most of England's woods and copses were planted as homes for foxes and pheasants), Game-birds and Etiquette. After luncheon, the students shoot some clays to get their eye in, and to give Robin some idea of what he has got on his plate. Then, if the weather be fine, you can light your pipe and go and cast a fly for one of the wily Fordley trout. I wish you better luck than I had.

At dinner the students meet the guns who will be shooting

with them the next day. The plan is always to have a mix of experienced guns with the newcomers. In addition, every student will be accompanied by a 'minder', an experienced person who will advise, encourage and reprimand if necessary.

The second day is the shoot. On my visit, it was a day of cloud and sun, a pleasant breeze and time to admire the colours of a Suffolk autumn. Then the tension increased as the tapping of the beaters' sticks got louder. Check the gun for the umpteenth time. The first bird exploded from the hedge on my right: too low, there was a beater crouched in that hedge. More low birds (it was a bit early in the season) to ignore; now a good old cock, curling as he came. Bang! '****': pivot, sun in the eyes. Bang! He crumpled in the air, shot clean: my first Suffolk pheasant.

At present the course only offers five drives, followed by luncheon and a discussion, but Robin is considering expanding to a full day's shooting. As it is, it is a highly valuable course for any New Gun. No one can learn it all in two days, but people who attend the happy course at Fordley Hall must go away with a better appreciation of the countryside and the part that shooting plays in it. They will also go away with a brace of pheasants.

# Chapter Twenty-one

# CLEARANCES: OLD AND NEW

THERE IS A barren and beautiful peninsula in the west of Scotland, where I go on occasion. There are a few scattered crofts at the mainland end, but the broad edge that butts into the sea is empty, but for deer, eagles and ravens. It was not always like this. In the little valleys that run from the hills down to the sea, the tumbled walls of little settlements can be seen, and there are still traces of rig and furrow cultivation. There were once some 500 people living on this ten miles of coastline. They fished. They grew some oats, barley and potatoes. They made some whisky for their greater ease. Their main cash-crop came from the sale of their little black long-horned Kylie cattle (now you know where the name comes from). This hard and simple way of life was broken with the Clans at Culloden, and killed by the 'Clearances'.

There are two ways of looking at the Clearances. One view is that the lairds and the incoming English landlords found they could make more money by clearing the people out of the glens and filling them with sheep instead. The other view was that the people of the glens lived in 'poverty, squalor and slothful indolence, and thus their eviction and their enforced employment in fruitful industry elsewhere should be the Christian duty of their superiors'.

You may take your pick of these, but the facts are that many people were driven from their homes by force, packed in 'coffin ships' and sent off to Canada, or Australia; or they were left to drift into the slums of Glasgow. It is hard to look at those pathetic ruins without feeling a deep sympathy for those simple people and their loss. It is easy, and fashionable, to allow oneself a little self-righteous anger at those who caused it to happen, especially as it is all comfortably in the past; or is it?

We all know how difficult it is for young people in rural areas to find a home. Now just suppose I live in a village and I want to sell my house. Am I going to offer it to a deserving young local couple at a price that they can afford? No, I am going to get the best price I can for it, which means that it will probably be bought by a 'white settler'. This may mean that the young people will have to move away from their family and their roots. They will, in effect, have been evicted from their community. Of course it is my duty to my family to 'maximize the return on my asset', but there is the nagging thought that the difference between me and the laird clearing his glen might just be one of degree and not of principle.

I am in the process of selling my ewes. This has not been an easy decision, because sheep have been part of my way of life for a long time. However, they are also a business. I have always kept sheep with a view to my sheep helping to keep me. I can see no prospect of profit in the foreseeable future. My little farm has never given me full-time employment, but I worked hard at it, enjoying my work. I managed to keep the bank happy, and have made a small contribution to the rural economy. It now seems fortunate that I ignored the exhortations of successive Ministers of Agriculture to expand, invest and produce more.

Because I do not depend on farming for my whole livelihood, I shall survive (God willing), and continue to live in my own home. Others will not be so lucky. An indiscreet local bank manager was heard to say that he reckoned forty per cent of his farming clients would be out of business within two years. In many cases they will also lose their homes and the only life that they have ever known. This is the price they will have to pay for listening to the politicians.

The Indigenous Countryman is under attack from all sides. He is a simple chap who wants to get on with his job of growing food for a reasonable return. He is a traditionalist. He wants to keep his way of life and mind his own business, without interruptions from a lot of interfering prodnoses. He does not understand why the world has suddenly turned against him: surely people want to eat? Poor chap, history is about to dump on him, just as it did on the wretched Highlanders. Politicians know that the rural vote is less than five per cent, and so the wrecking of rural life can proceed with minimal political damage. Indeed, politicians from all sides see the clearance of the Indigenous Countryman as thoroughly desirable. Countrymen have reactionary views and brutish habits (all that beastly hunting and shooting); they have no place in the brave new plastic Britain. The supermarket shelves can be filled with cheap food from Eastern Europe. The countryside can be turned into a nice derelict National Theme Park, where people can ramble, twitch and scatter litter at will.

It should not require much of a moral convulsion for Urban Man to convince himself that 'the eviction and enforced employment elsewhere' of the English Countryman is indeed meet, right, and a Christian Duty.

Chapter Twenty-two

# NO ONE CAN TELL WEATHER, OR NO

A RE WE GOING to have a hard winter? Many newspapers have called in their tame weather prophets. Some of these creatures have appeared on television, brandishing fir cones and bits of seaweed to show that they are the real thing. The burthen of their song is that we are in for a hard time. Maybe we are and maybe we are not. The one certain thing is that most of these folksy experts are false prophets: they know no more than you or I what the weather is going to be in the long-term. I remember one of the best known of these witch doctors forecasting a mild, wet winter, a few years ago; we had iron frost for six weeks. The same hero forecast a wet summer in 1990. I suppose he could argue that his forecast was correct in the west of Scotland, where they had had one hundred inches of rain by the end of September, but he would be clinging to the rags of his reputation. It is worthy of note that a famous Scottish wiseman, the Brahan Seer, predicted that the Western Highlands would one day become too wet for man or beast to inhabit. The Brahan Seer's record to date has shown a high scoring rate. However, unless you are blessed with second sight, it is impossible to make a long-term weather forecast. The good old British weather will usually confound those with the temerity to attempt to forecast it: ask that Nice Mr Fish.

Forget about the heavy crop of berries meaning a hard winter. A heavy crop of berries simply means that it has been a good season for berries. Certain natural indications can give an idea of likely local weather conditions, but they will be strictly local (like in the Parish), and strictly short-term (a month at the very most).

One of the more reliable bits of weather lore is the rhyme about 'if ice in November holds a duck, February will be slush and muck'. A cold snap in November can often presage a mild, wet winter. There was certainly a cold snap in north Northumberland in the latter part of November. There was a quarry lorry embedded in the wall of the old smithy in the village the other morning, and the Major's car slid sideways all the way down the hill. I could not find a cooperative duck to test the ice on the pond, but it certainly held a terrier (if not a Rottweiler).

The local tradition is that if Cheviot is seen to be covered in snow three times in November (it was), then the rest of the winter is likely to be mild, which is another version of the 'slush and muck' theory. They have a similar theory about the North York Moors. 'The white cow's slipped her calf,' the locals say with satisfaction, looking up at the white tops, but it does not always work. The 'White Cow' sometimes comes bellowing back with a vengeance. I have heard people enthusing about the beauty of the snow-covered countryside. They tend to be people who do not have half a mile of track to plough out, and who do not have to wade through the stuff to feed hungry sheep. Snow is best on Christmas cards. At least you do not have to shovel rain.

The moon is important for do-it-yourself weather forecasting. The weather that prevails over a new moon is likely to set the pattern until the next new moon. Any change within that time is most likely to occur around the full moon. A halo round the moon usually means a change in the weather. The poor old moon is little regarded these days. Our forefathers understood the importance of her influence; after all, the tides work with the moon, so why not the weather? Everything in nature slots into everything else. Modern man would do well to remember that fact.

The wind is obviously all-important. Nothing good ever came out of the east, and that certainly applies to weather. All the really nasty, mean, bone-chilling, mind-numbing stuff in this part of the world comes out of the south-east: it is a 'bad

airt' (direction). Anyone who wants to read a political statement into this is welcome to do so. Thank goodness that our
prevailing wind is westerly. The way the wind changes is
important. It is best if the wind 'veers' (changes clockwise). A
wind that 'backs' (anti-clockwise) can be brewing up something
nasty.

Some animals are good weather prophets. There used to be
a lot of Galloway cows on Dartmoor when I was a young
man. On occasion you would see long lines of shaggy black
cattle filing down off the high moor. It was a certain sign of
snow on the way.

So are we going to have a hard winter? The only absolute
certainty is that no one knows for certain. Let the prophets
prophesy: by the law of averages they are bound to get it
right eventually. Sensible folk will hope for the best, prepare
for the worst, and take what is sent.

# Chapter Twenty-three

# OF COURSE IT'S PURE COINCIDENCE, BUT . . .

FOR MOST OF my life I have loved and hunted foxes. Should you have a problem with this statement, then the problem is yours and not mine. It is a fact that man can only hunt an animal successfully if he has an affinity with that animal and understands it fully. It is impossible to understand an animal properly without coming to love it. Our ancient forebears understood this thoroughly. Indeed they went further: they considered that the soul of the hunter and the hunted were somehow interconnected. Nonsense? Maybe, but those who mix much with nature know that there are things that defy rational explanation. They do not always talk about these things for fear of the very ridicule which some of you are already brewing up.

There has certainly always been something a bit 'uncanny' about foxes, and there have been many tales of strange happenings through the ages. I am going to tell you just three that happened in the present century.

The Earl of Harrington was Master of his own hounds from 1881–1917. He hunted the country which is now hunted by the South Notts Hunt. The Earl was a big man, and it is important to remember that he had an enormous grey beard. He left a stipulation in his will that, were he to die during the hunting season, then hounds were to meet at a certain place on the first convenient day after the funeral and were to draw a certain covert.

The old man's wish was duly honoured. Hounds met and were taken to the covert, and, so the story goes, went away on a huge grey fox. A fast hunt followed, in which hounds outstripped the followers. They found hounds standing on Lord Harrington's grave. Fred Earp, the huntsman, removed his cap and said: 'Well, gentlemen, I am going home; His Lordship has called his hounds.'

Robin Hill (1871–1958) lived at Low Hall, Brompton, in North Yorkshire. He lived for foxhunting with the Derwent and the Sinnington hunts, but towards the end of his life he suffered a long illness that prevented him from hunting. He was often heard to say that he longed for one more good day with hounds: 'And if I die without it, I shall come back as a fox and give them one good chase.' Robin Hill was buried at Brompton on 4 November. On 5 November, the Sinnington held their opening meet at the village from which the hunt took its name.

The day started badly, then as hounds were being taken through a rough, thorn-bushy field near Riseborough, a fox jumped up. This fox set his mask straight for the east, crossing into the Derwent country over the River Costa, which caused the followers to lose touch with the pack. Without going into too much local detail, it is sufficient to say that hounds kept heading east and towards Brompton. Not far from Brompton, hounds changed on to a fresh fox in the gathering dusk, but at the same time, a tired and obviously well-hunted fox was seen climbing the wall into Brompton cemetery. This was a hunt with a point of over ten miles and much more as hounds had run. It was a most unusual line for any fox to take, but a 'good chase' just as Robin Hill had promised.

Major Gerald Gundry was my stepfather-in-law. He was stubborn, charming, maddening and amusing; a rock steady friend and a redoubtable opponent; those who did not love him, respected him. A great part of his life was devoted to the Duke of Beaufort's Hunt. He was Joint Master with the late Duke from 1951 to 1985, and for nearly quarter of a century he hunted the doghounds. Everybody knew 'The Major'. The Beaufort Hounds and foxes were his passion. He was indeed a 'mighty hunter before the Lord'.

On 20 December 1990, at 3.25 p.m., Major Gundry died, aged seventy-nine. On 22 December 1990, the Duke of Beaufort's Hounds met at Foxley Green. Little was done in the morning, but in the early afternoon they found a fox and had a slow, circular hunt of some two hours. At exactly 3.25 p.m. hounds killed the fox at the Major's front door.

The man who told me this said: 'I am not an imaginative chap, but I do not mind telling you that I felt chills down my spine. There was a very strange feeling. Several people burst into tears.' So there you are: make of this what you will. 'Coincidence', some may say; is there such a thing? I do not pretend to know. All I know is that at the end of a day's hunting it is customary to thank the Master and wish him good night, so it can do no harm to say: 'Thank you, Major and good night.'

Chapter Twenty-four

# OF WATCHING THE LADY, YOUR WALLET AND YOUR BACK

APPLEBY-IN-WESTMORLAND is a pretty little town on the banks of the River Eden. For a few days in June every year the town is taken over by horses. James II granted the original charter to hold the horse fair at Appleby. The fair used to take place in the main street of the town. For reasons which may become apparent, this ceased to be acceptable. The police now close off a section of quiet back road about a mile outside the town; it is here that the business end of the fair operates, amongst fields full of lorries, caravans and pick-up trucks. The business of the fair is buying and selling horses; and harness and dogs and birds and carts and probably other things you are better not knowing about.

Should you be in search of a hunter for Leicestershire, or a future winner of the Cheltenham Gold Cup, then Appleby is not for you. You may well find your dream of a harness racer or a jolly skewbald to pull your brightly coloured trotter's cart. But be careful: you are not amongst the Church Lads' Brigade, and your Dream Horse might become a Nightmare: *Caveat Emptor* is the motto of Appleby Horse Fair. Appleby Fair is really part of the closed world of the travelling people: Romanies, didicoys and tinkers. Outsiders may be well advised to stick to gawping and photography.

Along the side road there are lorries selling harness and other equine necessities. Rows of horses are tethered to the hedges on either side. Lines of men with shuttered faces and watchful eyes sit on the grassy banks. Some of the faces bear traces of recent arguments of a non-intellectual nature.

The lane is thronged with slowly moving crowds of people. Hi! Hi! Hi!'; the crowd parts swiftly to allow the passage of a furiously driven trotter, pulling a sulky (light two-wheeled cart, used in harness racing). It is definitely caveat pedestrian here too.

On the trodden verges hot-dog and fish 'n' chip vans do their bit for the atmosphere, which starts to thicken with the crowd; rancid cooking grease, hair oil, cheap scent and aggressive armpits mingle with horse sweat and trampled dung to create an interesting olfactory experience.

A Shetland pony with a tiny and beautifully painted cart stands by the road. A camera-bristling tourist wants a picture. A small tousled boy clutching a shillelagh as big as himself is cajoled to sit on the cart: 'Will youse get on the cart now, Tommy, and let the man get a foty.'

'Hey up! hey up!' The same furious trotter and his long-haired driver bursts through the crowd again. He is followed at a more leisurely pace by a man riding one piebald cob and leading another, with fourteen other piebalds following loose behind.

There is a roadside caravan covered in primitive oil paintings of rural scenes. There are dogs everywhere amongst the crowd, mostly lurchers. There are two pit bull terriers, only puppies, but already with a no-nonsense look about them.

'What you use them for, then?'

'Rabbits'; the blinds come down on the surrounding faces.

The pungent smell of burning hoof tells of the presence of the farrier. He has a handy, gas-fired travelling forge in the back of his van. He is trying to shoe a reluctant Dales pony. At last, with two men at the head and two more hanging on to its tail, it stands still.

Further down the lane is a quiet, neat little bungalow: a cattery. One cannot help wondering how they welcome the influx of temporary neighbours, but they are not opening their door to anybody. The first sighting of a traditional wooden caravan, beautifully painted and ornamented, is made, but it is roped firmly on top of a modern four-wheeled trailer. A four-day-old foal is taking luncheon.

The tempo and the temperature are warming up. The crowd suddenly thickens. There are raised voices and a flurry of fists. The police are swiftly through the throng, and a large (very large) sergeant is between the protagonists and speaking words of sweet reason to them. They are led away by their respective clans, but come to blows again a few yards up the road. 'Hi! Hi! Hi! Watch yer backs!' The fight and the crowd scatter for another furiously driven sulky. A man with a bleeding face is plonked on a cart and driven away.

The three-card men are on the job, working on the top of cardboard boxes (easily rendered innocent should the 'polis' come along): 'That's the Lady: that's the prize;' he flicks the cards over and back showing two tens. 'Those you lose. Now fifty down to win a hundred; who'll bet fifty?' A fat man puts down fifty and turns up the Queen. He gets his hundred. Bets again: wins again. It looks easy: too easy. The Fat Man could not be an accomplice, could be? That would be dishonest. . . .

The pace of the trotting is furious and almost continuous now. Some are trying to race two abreast down the narrow road. 'Oh, there'll be sich a smash in a minute,' says an old man leaning on a stick. 'Why, there was a woman killt yesterday. But the lads were sharp, mind. They had a policeman hold a horse to keep him busy, whilst they got the body quick out the way and no one looking.'

Down in the town, boys ride their horses into the deep river pools below the bridge, to wash them off. The pubs brim over on to the pavements. A dirty girl asks for money for a fiddler and penny whistler. They seem more like middle-class mendicants than travellers. The concertina player with the weathered face and a cheerful-looking corgi dog sitting in a basket beside him gets my money: he seems more right for Appleby.

Chapter Twenty-five

# IN WHICH THE BURRA SAHIB MUSES ON TRAVEL AND BATHES AN ELEPHANT

INDIA IS A Travellers' rather than a Tourists' country. It is especially for those who like the challenge of travelling hopefully, and are not too worried about the fine details of arrivals. Internal flights are reasonable and cheap, but there may be a relaxed approach to timetables. This is all part of the adventure.

Some will say that rail is the only way to travel in India: 'Up to a point, Lord Copper'. Many people would find air-conditioned First Class acceptable; more or less. AC1 tends to be booked up at least two months ahead, and is not available on all trains. There are always a couple of AC1 compartments kept for VIP allocation. How you work that one out is up to you.

Indian driving is best left to the Indians. Everybody drives in the middle of the road, the sides being full of pedestrians and bullock carts. Strong nerves, good brakes and a robust horn are needed. You will be amazed that there are not more accidents, until you learn that a driver who hits somebody (or, much worse, a cow) is liable for immediate lynching.

It is a good idea to learn a few basic phrases in Hindi (the official language). I did have an old Army phrase book in my knapsack, but found little use for phrases such as 'Corporal, that mule's sheath is filthy', or 'That saddle will gall the wither'. Most educated Indians speak English, even amongst themselves, but the majority of the population do not. There are two bits of English which are in common usage: 'Hello' is a plea for money; 'No problem' is the universal answer to a request. The taxi driver you have asked to take you to the 'Bubblipur Hilton' says 'No problem' because it is the only bit of English that he knows. He is going to take you to the Hotel Blue Moon whether you like it or not; the chances are that you will not.

To be White, Large and Male can still be advantageous, especially in rural India. However, should you be Blonde, Young, Pretty and Female, you should think twice about travelling on your own, and should make sure that your door locks.

Indian Bureaucracy must rank amongst the wonders of the world. Do not lose your temper, never shout, and take a good book with you. Something always gets done in the end. It may not be what you wanted, but there you go. A fifty-rupee note can be a useful solvent. Friends with influence are best of all.

It is almost inevitable that your bowels will throw a wobbly. Take a vast supply of anti-dysentery pills. These must contain an antibiotic, however reluctant your doctor may be. Never have ice in your drinks, and use only bottled, or sterilized, water. Sterilized water tastes filthy, but the average 'Eastern Squatter' is filthier: the choice (and the necessity) is yours.

How do you bathe an elephant? It is quite simple, really. You take it down to the river, roll it over on its side, splash water over it and then scrub-a-dub-dub with a pumice stone. But first find your elephant. The place for that is India.

The Indian Government has a firm wildlife conservation policy. This is not always easy in a country where the pressures of increasing population are immense. One of the jewels of this policy is undoubtedly the Kanha National Park in Manha Pradesh. The Park covers 2,000 square kilometres, comprising an outer ring of forest where people are allowed to live under strict controls regarding grazing and wood cutting. The inner core of 1,000 square kilometres is closed to all except forest rangers and authorized visitors.

Anyone brought up on Kipling's *Jungle Books* will recognize these forested hills immediately. The forest varies from dense thickets of bamboo, through more open stretches of hard-woods, to open savannah. Here live chital, sambur, swamp deer, bison, black buck with the wonderful fluted horns, jackal, leopard, sloth bear and tiger; yes, you can still get yourself eaten by a tiger. The last person to be accorded this honour was English. He ignored instructions and wandered off into the forest. They found his legs.

There are still wolves in the north of the Park. Kipling called his wolves the Seoni Wolf Pack. Seoni does exist, about three hours' drive to the west of Kanha. Any forest that existed there has been burned, hacked and charcoaled; the land has become arid, eroded and barren: a stark and minatory contrast to Kanha.

There are several bases from which you may explore the forest. Kipling Camp belongs to Bob and Anne Wright, both redoubtable and both OBEs. They also run the famous Tolly-gunge Club in Calcutta, and an orphanage in Kalimpong. The camp is open through the cool season (November to March). Anne Wright describes the accommodation as 'basic', but 'spartan comfort' is more appropriate. There are double rooms, with attached shower room, in huts scattered around the wooded compound. Meals are in the central mess, presided over by the Head Bearer, the incomparable Nabi. The organization of the camp is always in the hands of two English girls, chosen for their cheerful resilience, resourcefulness and charm. Katie is in her second season at the camp, and Polly just starting her first. They are both young, but seasoned travellers, and both charming and amusing companions. Kipling Camp operates at a high level of morale and cheerful efficiency, which all travellers in India will find most welcome.

The day starts at 0530 with tea and hot water brought by well-muffled bearers. The early morning chill in the cool season is considerable, especially in the back of an open Land-Rover. There are various barriers ('Checkposts') to be negotiated on the way into the forest. At the last barrier you get issued with a guide. The Kipling Camp drivers know the reserve like their own homes, and some, like the ever-cheerful Bofati, are expert naturalists. The guide is obligatory: he is not for guiding, he is for 'being there'.

The early morning is the best time to see wildlife, which very sensibly gets its head down in the heat of the day. Fresh tiger pug-marks on the dirt road always cause excitement. The Sonf Meadow is a favourite place to stop for a coffee break. This wide expanse of grassland is not a natural meadow. It is the result of slash-and-burn agriculture by the Baiga. The Baiga were the aboriginal inhabitants of the forest, who were resettled outside the Park in 1969. Beside certain termite mounds in the forest you can still come across coconut shells and flowers, sad little offerings to the forest gods by the displaced people. The Sonf is covered in herds of chital, the little white-spotted deer, which is probably the most common animal in the forest. The meadow is also home for a herd of the much rarer swamp deer.

But what about the elephants? I am coming to them; please be a little patient. By about 10 o'clock the party will have made its way back to Kanha, stopping to see whatever may be seen on the way. It might be a huge sambur buck, still wet and reeking from a mud wallow. It might be jungle bison with huge sweeping horns. The antics and effortless trapeze expertise of the langur monkeys is always fascinating, and that big male scratching himself intimately looks just like. . . .

Kanha is the administrative centre of the Park. There is the guest house where Mrs Gandhi loved to stay. There are also the radio station and the elephant lines. All over the Park the mahouts will have been out at dawn on their elephants, looking for tiger signs. So at Kanha you sit and have your picnic breakfast and wait for any news of a sighting. In a negative-tiger situation, you can go for an elephant ride. The Park has some fourteen elephants. They do routine maintenance work, and also act as mobile viewing platforms. At the time of my visit several of the elephants had been trucked off to a park in Bihar. They were being used to drive off some wild elephants who were causing havoc in the surrounding farms.

An elephant is much the best way to see the forest. At a gentle swaying pace you cross swamps and rivers, climb hills and push through thickets. The wildlife totally ignores the passing elephant. Should a branch threaten the security of the Sahib's hat, Hemaviti, or Bund Debi, will reach up her trunk and remove it.

Should a tiger be reported, everybody drives off at high speed to the appropriate spot, where an elephant will be waiting. It might be Jung Bahadur, the huge forty-two-year-old tusker (elephants have the same age span as humans) who once, when in musth, soothed his sexual frenzy by wrecking three Land-Rovers. Sukhal Singth, J.B.'s mahout, climbs aboard by running up an extended foreleg and swinging up on an ear. The fatter sort of sahib is given a bamboo ladder.

Meanwhile, out in the forest, the tiger is being watched by two other elephants and their mahouts. The tigers seem to pay no attention to the elephants, or the mahouts, who communicate by whistles and shrill cries. There she is! Where? Under that tree; can you not see? No, not at once. So perfect is the tiger's camouflage that she is totally hidden by the shadow and the thin underbrush. The shape emerges gradually. A large tigress, sleepy, replete and pregnant, stretched out like a huge contented pussy cat; only a watchful eye shows that she knows we are there. This is no good. The Indian gentleman with a ciné-camera wants a bit of action. Jung Bahadur plucks up a small dead tree with his trunk and waggles it about. The tigress obliges by moving twenty yards and curling up under a tree. 'Shabash!' (well done), we all say to the mahouts, as we head back. They are beside themselves with delight.

Kipling Camp is also the home of Tara. Tara is the elephant on which Mark Shand, the eminent traveller, did his three-month trek across part of India. Thus it came to pass one evening that we set off to the river; the 'we' being Tara, the Memsahib and I, Tahid, the second mahout (who was driving), and Mujhim (the head mahout) walking behind and directing operations. It was Tara's bath time. By the way, you drive an elephant with your toes, kicking and wiggling behind the ears. On occasion you fetch it a hefty whack over the head with your stick and shout something that might be 'Hai!' at it.

At the river the elephant lies down, the Sahib is rebuked for jumping off the side instead of sliding off over the tail as any civilized person would, then the howdah is removed. Tara stands up, curls her trunk and Tahid runs up it on to her head and rides her into the river, where she rolls over on to her near side and the scrubbing begins. Both sides are scrubbed, every nook and cranny, even between the toenails. There is an awful lot of elephant. All the time Tara blows, bubbles and splashes with her trunk. She then dries off in the sun and is resaddled. She curls her tail on command to make a convenient mounting step. It is necessary to hang on very tightly as she gets to her feet. Then comes the pleasant rolling ride home through the dusk.

Back at the camp and dismounted I raise my hat to Tara as one should to a lady. Mujhim bids her to 'Salaam to the Sahib'. Tara raises her trunk in the elephant's salute, then lowers it, trumpets loudly and covers me in elephant snot: Shabash, Tara.

# Chapter Twenty-six

# CHRISTMAS COMES BUT ONCE A YEAR

O VER 1,000,000 PEOPLE (including myself) attended the Boxing Day meet of their local hunt this year. Boxing Day is a great occasion, a festive day, a hunting holiday, when the Goodwill is often better than the Hunting. Every vantage point and byway becomes clogged with enthusiasts, whose eagerness can impede the progress of what is, after all, a wild sport. Foxhunting does not come much wilder than it does in the rugged hills of the English/Scottish Border country. This is the land of 'nine months' winter and three months' bad weather'; the land of isolated farms and steadings where there are no 'main services', and the hardy inhabitants keep well-stocked store cupboards against being 'blocked in'.

For generations the working and social life of the hills has revolved around sheep and foxhunting. Let there be no mis-understanding: for the hillmen, the purpose of the local pack of hounds is to kill foxes. The hill fox likes lamb on his menu, and this brings him into dispute with men for whom their lamb crop is their livelihood. But let this also be understood: it would not be difficult to destroy the hill foxes. The shepherds know where they breed and could easily wipe out the cubs. But we are not murderers; we want control, not holocaust. For us the hounds are the traditional way, the fair way and the natural way. We love watching and listening to the hounds and we like to see the fox well hunted and fairly caught. We enjoy the excitement of trying to keep in touch with the fast-running pack (a hill hound may cover one hundred miles, and more, in a hunting day). Should hounds catch the fox, we rejoice in a fitting climax to the hunt. Should the fox escape we wish him luck as a hardy opponent. Some people may have difficulty with this philosophy but that is their problem. To us hunting is as natural a part of life as is eating, sleeping and breathing; and just about as important.

We might be a bit short on the fashionable frills. The screaming hill winds do not like top hats. As you can see, we dress for comfort and convenience in hard conditions. In fact we tend to wear our working clothes, because many of us have ridden over the hills straight from the morning rounds of flocks and herds. In days gone by, those rounds would likely have been done on horses. The men of the Borders are descendants of the famous 'Riding Clans', who lived by raiding and reiving. The shepherding horse has now been mainly replaced by the amazing ATV, 'the biggest advance in sheep farming since the collie dog'. This now indispensable hill farmer's workhorse adapts well to hunting: it never gets tired, does not go lame and skims across the boggy peat haggs, where a horse would sink with all hands.

We sat our mechanized mounts on the hill top. In the bitter winter sunshine the great hills rolled away in varying shades of green and black and brown.

'Man, did ye ever see a bonnier view than yon?'

Below us the moving white dots of the hounds were spread out in a big patch of russet bracken. A single hound spoke, then a swelling chorus of wild, thrilling hound voices.

'He's yonder, look!' And there was the lithe brown shape sliding over the old stone dyke at the bottom of the valley, 600 feet below.

'It's a damn sight bonnier view with hoonds and a fox in it!'

Amen to that! say I.


Most of my life has been lived in a succession of large Victorian houses. These houses were so designed that a posse of servants was required to maintain the inmates in anything approximating to comfort. The primitive central heating systems were usually driven by a Moloch of a furnace that consumed more fuel in a day than the Great Western Railway

Even then it barely managed to keep the temperature above freezing. Normal life in the winter for me meant wearing several sweaters with a quilted jacket, and bolting from the stove-warm kitchen to the one room where a decent fire was permitted. I have very often driven my word processor whilst wearing mittens.

Five years ago I rebelled against the tradition of a lifetime, and had built for me and mine a small, snug, single-storey dwelling. It has double glazing, central heating, a Norwegian stove and an eerie lack of draughts. It is *warm*. The result of this is that I have become soft. I have just returned from a week on the west coast of Scotland. The house where I stayed was built in 1850. There is no heating. The roof leaks when the great Atlantic gales come whooping across Mull and hit the house head on. For a couple of days I cursed and shivered and shaved fully dressed. By the end of the week I was happily back in the old routine of toasting my feet in front of the fire, whilst turning my twice-sweatered, quilted-waistcoat-clad back to the draughts that swept across the wasteland of the drawing room. It was just like the old days — but it was nice to get home.

# Chapter Twenty-seven

# 'IT'S REALLY MUCH THE SAME IN FRANCE'

*Dedicated to my good friends Hubert and Odette Chevallier-Chantepie, who were killed in a tragic accident in November 1991, and all their family.*

'Go,' I WAS TOLD, 'and see how different a French farmer is: how many heads; that sort of thing.'

Stick a pin in the middle of a map of France and it will find the Bourbonnais: the rural heartland. This is *'France Profonde'*. It is gently rolling countryside of small stock farms and huge oak woods. The oak woods are managed on a centuries-old coppicing system that produces a constant supply of firewood and superb mature timber. These woods also support a chain of wild life such as has been largely destroyed in this country. France does not have the pressures of population that we have in Britain. This means that miles of unpaved road still ramble in a tranquil manner through 'unimproved' farmland. There are still frogs to hop across these roads. Dogs can lie in the sun in the middle of the village street, which is also the favourite place for those endless and passionate conversations that are the fuel of French life.

You can still stand outside the door drinking an early cup of coffee and hear a woodpecker hard at work in the wood. It is a very long time since I heard a woodpecker in England. My wife summed it up. She said that it was like England used to be when we were both children. It is only when you go somewhere like the Bourbonnais that you realize just how much of rural England has been destroyed and damaged: I suspect that much of the damage is now beyond repair.

A little road winds across one of the numerous small valleys with their secret streams and climbs to a tiny hill-top village grouped round an ancient chateau (it is now owned by a Socialist millionaire 'who wishes everybody to be poor except for himself and M Mitterrand'). Turn right and there is an unpaved road that eventually seems determined to lose itself in an oak wood. Go just a little further and there is La Foitière, the home of the Chevallier-Chantepie family. 'Gentleman Farmer' is a description of respectable currency in France. The CCs (as they are locally known) are of *ancienne famille*. The modern family consists of M Hubert, Mme Odette, Sophie (twenty), Guillaume (eighteen), Aude (fourteen) and *Les Jumelles* (identical), Isabelle and Veronique (twelve).

La Foitière has been in Hubert's mother's family since 13something. On the male line he comes down from the famous Vingt-quatre Barbres who got his name on a crusade in Spain when he totalled twenty-four bearded Moors before *déjeuner*. The family have continued the military tradition: Hubert's father is a retired General, and his younger brother a serving Lt. Colonel.

The property is farmed in partnership between Hubert and his father, and amounts to some 470 acres (190 hectares). The farmhouse is a long, seventeenth-century house, one room thick. It was a noisome ruin when the CCs took over the farm twenty years ago. They have restored it bit by bit and with their own hands. It is now the sort of comfortable, dog-and-child-scarred country house where a visiting Englishman feels very much at home.

Hubert grows 150 acres (60 hectares) of arable crops: wheat, sunflowers and rape, which he rotates with 75 acres (30 hectares) of grass leys. The rest of the farm is permanent pasture for his pride and his glory: his eighty-cow suckler herd of pure-bred Charollais. This is the heartland of the white Charollais cattle, and beef production is the main enterprise of the area. The La Foitière cows calve down in February and March. The bull calves are sold in December/January at 350–400 kgs. Twenty of the best heifer calves are kept for replacements; the rest are sold at eighteen to thirty months old for meat or breeding.

No full-time labour is now used on La Foitière; thirty years ago there were fifteen full-time workers. The French farm worker is virtually extinct since the Socialist government imposed a social security tax of fifty per cent of a worker's wage. This has lead to widespread unemployment, not just in agriculture. Hubert has developed a system whereby he can do most things himself and from a tractor. The cows are wintered in a large airy shed in pens of twenty. At the back of the shed is a feed barrier and passage. The morning ration of concentrate is poured along one side of the rails, and the cows stick their heads through. The push of a lever closes the barrier so that the cows are yoked. This means that whilst the cows are feeding, work in the pens (bedding up, filling the hay racks, injecting calves and so forth) can continue with minimum disturbance. Under the French system, cattle are accustomed to being handled and tied up from a very early age. This makes them extremely docile. It is fashionable in England to say that the French are bad with animals. It is certainly true that the French regard an animal as an animal, not as a human being in a furry coat. At all the farms I visited the standards of stockmanship were very high.

After the 6.30 feed, Hubert drives across for his daily inspection of his father's farm. (A parenthesis on the agricultural motor car: unlike some of their British counterparts, French farmers are not impressed by the car as a status symbol. French agricultural cars rattle, bang, wheeze and shudder; occasionally bits fall off. No one minds very much and they usually get there; rather fast.) The farm lies on two sides of a valley. There are woodlands with roe deer, pheasants and woodcock. There are ponds on the little river stocked with carp and pike. In the middle of the farm is a roadstone quarry, which must help the general economics.

Father C C winters in the south for his health. His house is a delightful *petit château* built round three sides of a courtyard. The oldest part is fourteenth century. It was renovated in 1650.

After *petit déjeuner* we visited Hubert's neighbours, the Fradens (father — Fernand, and son — Bernard). Fernand was originally a tenant farmer, but managed to buy his farm and eventually a neighbouring one as well. They are hardworking, quiet people, with obvious pride in their Charollais herd. After inspecting the cows, we were soon in the neat kitchen with a bottle of Rivesalte, fortified Muscat wine. 'Tell them,' said Fernand, 'that farming is bad in France. It is a catastrophe.'

As in England, the French farmers feel that the politicians have done the dirty on them. The saying is that politicians 'have the heads of Arabs': this is not meant as a compliment. The Peasants (the word is normal usage) are being driven from the land. Cheap meat is being allowed in from Eastern Europe for political reasons, ruining the native beef trade.

'Ah ha!' the visitor might say (as his glass was topped up yet again), 'but you have a cheap interest rate ...' (four to nine per cent for farmers).

'But no, to borrow money is a catastrophe, and then in France there is land tax and building tax and the capital taxes are a crime enormous.' It all had a pretty familiar ring to it, but then another bottle of Rivesalte appeared and the conversation turned to *La Chasse*. That night we dined with the Lady Master of the local boar hounds (potato tart, pheasant, salad, cheese, excellent Corsican wine). She is also a sheep farmer. We always have great arguments, because she uses Suffolk (English) rams, whilst I use Bleu du Maine (French). Sheep farming is a mutual disaster area, however, so we talked about hunting instead.

The next day was Saturday. In the quieter time of winter many farmers in France go hunting. Saturday is boar hunting. A bull calf appeared at about 3.00 a.m., and was well and sucking strongly. By 7.00 a.m. everything was fed, and Hubert and I were on the road to *Faire le Bois*. Wild pig are nocturnal feeders and cover a large area in a night. It is necessary to find out, from footprints and other signs, which stretch of woodland they are lying up in for the day.

We were on the estate of M Henri de Villette, one of the largest landowners in the area. We found no recent signs of pig. By 10.30 everybody had foregathered for a substantial *déjeuner* at an *auberge*. Mayeul had found some pig, and everybody was happy except with the weather. The previous week there had been two feet of snow; now it was dry, with a cloudless sky and the temperature in the high sixties: not good for hunting. So it proved to be. It got hotter, the scent disappeared, and the day ground to a halt in a welter of roadside discussions animated by disappointment.

It is the custom after hunting in France that there is always a dinner: sometimes *grand*, sometimes *petit*; sometimes in an *auberge*, sometimes in a house. The CCs sat seventy people down to dinner that night. Madame and the girls had done the whole thing (onion tart, chicken in aspic, salad, cheese, chocolate mousse), from a kitchen the size of a trawler galley.

It has been said that the French drink a lot, but their real fix is Talk. Wine is a helpful lubricant. It turns French from a fast-flowing language into a spate. A subject is selected, dissected, analysed, discarded. The talk whirls and froths and then picks up the same subject and takes another dash downstream with it. A visiting Englishman with a rather plain command of French is quickly drowned in the flood.

Sunday brought a little lie-in, and the calf of that night co-operated by not arriving until 6.00 a.m. The after-Mass calm of a Sabbath morning was pierced by a noise of such force and intensity that they must have been able to hear it in Jaligny-sur-Besbre. This sort of noise can only be produced by a *jumelle* who has been tricked into being tied to a tree by a perfidious other half, and then abandoned. It was suggested to Odette that there might be some interesting times with the twins in years to come. She raised her eyes to Heaven.

This was to be another busy day. It was the day of the Roe Shoot. This was not sport, but business. In each area there is a commission of farmers, foresters, sportsmen and government officials. They determine how many roe deer are to be culled on each property in their area. The owner is then legally obliged to carry out this cull before the end of February, and to produce carcases with official tags as proof. Hubert still had two deer to get, so three CC brothers, together with assorted friends, wives, children and dogs descended on La Foitière.

Each wood was driven with much shouting, horn-blowing and excited barking to where a line of guns (armed with an assortment of ball-loaded shotguns and rifles) lay in wait. As yet another burst of fire swept the countryside, I could not but ponder on the likely reactions of our own dear Ramblers' Association. They do not seem to have ramblers in France: perhaps they have all been culled. However, by the end of the day Hubert's cull had been fulfilled. A happy family gathering tucked into *Le Whisky*. Then it was a quick change and out to dinner (pizza, choucroute, salad, cheese, orange tart), with the Comtesse de Linery, an eminent local author and historian.

The next day brought another lovely morning, with once again the promise of high temperatures. There was no calf in the night. Monday morning is when Hubert puts the week's supply of hay in the pens, driving in and out whilst the cows are yoked up. The hay is fed *ad lib*, and comes in big round bales. It was the most lovely hay, every handful full of the scents of summer. The Bourbonnais hay time in June is one of almost guaranteed sun and breeze; their hay should be good.

To Coopaca (Coopérative Agricole de Céréales et d'Approvisionments): the farm co-operative system is big in France; seventy per cent of French farmers belong to a co-op, through which they sell their produce and buy their seed, fertilizer, *et al*. This local co-op is one of a group of four; Hubert is on the Finance Committee. The huge premises with its silos and warehouses seemed very well organized. My French struggled a bit with farm finance, but it does seem as though French arable prices are pretty much the same as those in the UK.

Stanislaus de Villette is the eldest son of M Henri. He is also one of the biggest sheep farmers in that part of France. Stan spent a year in Scotland, farming when he was not shooting and vice versa. He runs 2,000 ewes of which 1,600 are housed in British pattern houses. There are three sheds 100 metres long by 12 wide. The ewes are clipped and housed in early January. They lamb in 5 lots from January to May, with lambs being sold at 12–16 weeks. The ewes and lambs looked bright-faced and well. What sort of ewes? 'De Villette' says Stanislaus. He has developed his own type from Suffolk × Ile de France × Charollais × Finn and breeds all his own replacement ewes.

The Bourbonnais is dotted with little chateaux, each with a tale of some perfidy committed by the English 'Goddams' during the Hundred Years War, the memory of which seems still fresh, if not fragrant. Almost all the chateaux seem to be inhabited by Hubert's cousins. We visited a cousin.

This cousin keeps his cows on the traditional system, neck-chained in their stalls during the winter. All the feeding is done by hand down a central passage. There is another passage behind the tethered cow where the calves appear and the waste products are dealt with. Everything is done manually except for the conveyor belt. This sytem is a great feature of the older cow sheds. It is a continuous belt built into the floor of the building. You fork all the waste products on to the belt and away it chugs out through a hole on the wall, up a gantry and tips on to the muck heap: all rather jolly and much better than a wheelbarrow.

Monday night: a '*Grand Dîner*' (avocado, pheasant, apple pudding with 'sauce anglaise', which is custard; salad and cheese as always in France) with five couples of eminent *agriculteurs* plus their children. The state of French agriculture was comprehensively rehearsed with grand passion. The general impression was that French farming was crevé (knackered); by 0130 so was I.

Tuesday: no calves in the night.

'The cows keep a tight bottom,' said Odette.

'Today we go foxhunting,' said Hubert, to whom sleep is of little importance.

It actually turned out to be boar hunting when we got there, but the Rallye St Romain hunt either quarry with equal enthusiasm. Boar hunting is extremely exciting. There was a quick '*attaque*' and we had a good view of the hounds going away from a big wood. French hunts, of which there are over three hundred, have a tremendous car following. Now that I no longer ride I always hitch a lift with one of them. I have heard people in Britain complain that following hounds in a motor car is dull: they should experience the French version. The French car followers allow their Gallic zeal a very loose rein and maximum revs. I spent a lot of time with my eyes closed and my knuckles white with the effort of hanging on. Think of Le Mans x Auto Cross x Banger Racing; except that for some miraculous reason no one ever seems to hit anything. The French are neither patient, nor slow, in conducting a motor car at any time, but any normal constraints are cast aside when the passions of the chase are high. It can be an interesting experience.

We eventually halted at a crossroads in the forest. The heat was building up again. The cry of hounds came nearer, then three pigs came crashing across the ride: a thrilling sight. Hubert whipped out his *cour de chasse* from the car boot and blew *'Le Sanglier'* to indicate pig and *'Les Animaux en Compagnie'* to show that there was more than one. There are something like seventy different basic 'fanfares' from which an expert can tell exactly what is happening at any stage of a hunt.

Hounds lost the boar in the heat of the afternoon. So at 4.00 pm they drew for a fox instead. As the day got cooler they had a very spirited hunt from a wooded hill down into the open farmland below. The watchers on the hill had a great view of fox (*'Voilà Groupil!'*: the colloquial name for a fox) and hounds in the open country. The fox went to ground, and hounds departed to the strains of *'La Rentrée au Chenil'*.

On Wednesday we went to the Mart. This meant getting up at 0330 hrs. French livestock marts work early for the benefit of the German and Italian buyers. Sancoin claims to be the biggest livestock mart in Europe, although some British marts might dispute this. It is certainly the biggest in France, with some 9,000 fat cattle, store cattle, sheep, goats and horses being put through every Thursday morning.

Our guide was M Patrick Lamotte. Patrick is head buyer for SICAGIEB, an important cattle co-op, and, as such, a man of note at Sancoin. This was a good thing, because one soon gets the definite impression that casual visitors are not well regarded.

By 0500 the huge building was a blaring, bleating, shouting whirl of activity. The sale of store cattle was not meant to commence until 0700 (fat cattle at 0800, sheep at 0900), but I suspect that most of the business had been done long before.

It is all done privately. The vendor stands by his pen of cattle. The buyers come by, argue, pass, return again, argue again, '8,600 francs? Poof! Robbery!'; hands are spread in horror. A horny finger stabs a palm: 'Listen, my brave one, a snip, a bargain, a gift! you want my blood also?' So it goes until a bargain is struck. But what about getting your money? There is no guarantee, especially with the Italians, it seems. One answer is to use the services of a Market Commissioner. These men are self-employed, but licensed by the market. They will buy and sell for you at a very reasonable one per cent commission, and they guarantee payment. This means that they must be not only very good judges of livestock, but also of human nature.

It hardly needs saying that there were some superb beef animals on sale, nearly all Charollais. Early morning translingual mental arithmetic is not my strong point, but it would seem that the best beef was fetching something like £1 per kilo more than it would in England, and this price was fifty pence a kilo less than a year ago. Cheap beef is flooding in from Eastern Europe. Officially it is coming from East Germany, but . . . Poof! (spread your hands and shrug your shoulders): it is political.

Good-quality butcher lambs were selling for pretty much the same price as I get for mine after I have claimed the lamb premium. We discussed this with a butcher. Any discussion in France quickly becomes a public meeting. The butcher said that he could buy English lamb for half the price of French. The French said they were being ruined. I said that I was being ruined. The butcher also said that . . . but Poof! butchers always say that.

It was still only 0830 when we got back to the farm. Hubert thought that bacon and eggs would be a smashing idea. Odette, who had not expected us back, thought otherwise. A French domestic altercation is pretty much like an English one, only rather more so. Anyway, they were very good bacon and eggs, and as there was once again a calfless night, it seemed like a good idea to go boar hunting with the Rallye Chapeau.

The day started well, with no less than seven pigs in front

of hounds; a remarkable sight. The pigs very sensibly went
into the 10,000-acre Forêt de Briffaut, which has many thick
plantations of young conifers. The weather was once again
more suitable for the beach. We occasionally drove furiously
round the forest one way, only to meet another column of
chasseurs driving equally furiously the other way, with as little
effect. There would then be instant and passionate mid-road
conferences, and just the occasional sound of a hound somewhere in a 500-acre thicket. But there was wine and ham and
pâté and bread and sausage, and a sun-warmed bank to lie on;
you cannot always have a good day's hunting.

That night the dinner was at the chateau of the Comte and
Comtesse Benoist d'Azy: everybody in their hunting clothes,
children and dogs running about, wine flowing and a massive
*cassoulet* to provide sustenance and fibre. The talk flowed of
hounds, and horses, and farming, and racing, and cattle, and
scandal and the iniquities of the government. I sat and sipped
and listened and watched. I thought: 'Here I am 700 miles
from home in a strange country, with a strange language, and
yet all the things that I have seen and done in the last week
are basically well-worn and familiar. At all times I have felt at
ease and amongst friends. What is remarkable is not the difference between French and English country people, but the
similarity. The concerns and worries, the pleasures and pastimes are very much the same. But, on the whole, the French
eat better.'

# Chapter Twenty-eight

# DRIVING A FOUR-HORSEPOWER BOWMAN

How would you get on at the controls of a four-horse power carriage? We are talking real Horse Power here, not your Internal Combustion nonsense.

'Horse Driving' (which is the official British Horse Society title) is the fastest-growing equestrian sport. What are its attractions? The first is that it obviously involves horses, and the British are a horsy people. Doubters may like to chew on the fact that there are now more horses in Britain than there were in 1914. The second attraction is that it requires skill. The third is that age is no bar to success. Many of the best drivers today may be described as being past the prime of life. Many have been successful in other equestrian disciplines, from which 'age, vice and unsoundness' may now preclude them.

Prince Philip is the man who first brought competitive carriage driving to Britain. As President of the International Equestrian Federation he saw competitive trials in Europe, and was the driving force in getting the sport started here. Driving offered him a fresh chance to pursue his love of the horse, just when arthritis was beginning to make polo difficult.

Mention 'Driving' and the name of George Bowman is certain to crop up. George is one of the best-known men in the Driving world, and has often been amongst the medals at the World Championships. In 1990 he won every event he competed in, including the National Championship for the thirteenth time.

Bowman Senior had a farm, hard-by Penrith. He also kept

horses for hauling fish and timber. George started off working with his father, then went rodeo riding in Canada. He came back and set up in the scrap and demolition business, with show jumping as a recreation. A working accident crushed his pelvis and crippled his legs for a time. There would be no more riding; so in 1967 he took up Driving. As everybody does, he started with one horse, then a pair, and at last the four-in-hand. He began Coaching (non-competitive driving), bought the Sir Walter Scott Road Coach, and drove it on its old run from Manchester to Edinburgh. In 1972 he drove his first competition.

The Bowman stables are in the back streets of Penrith. Here was Young George, who will be competing in the Pairs World Championship at Windsor later this month (August). Waiting in their roomy loose boxes were the members of 'The Team': Baby and Tinker — the Leaders (front), and Billy and Victor — the Wheelers (back). They are 'Cumbrian Cobs' — Hackney x Dales pony — wiry, sharp little horses.

The immaculate Harness Room was a delight to the eyes and the nose. A few years ago it was nearly impossible to get a set of harness made. Saddlers and harness makers have reappeared like mushrooms. A new set of ordinary driving harness will cost around £1,000. Did you know that there are now twenty-six firms making carriages in Britain? George's competition carriage was made by a German company. The firm makes nothing else, and employs seventy-eight men working on shifts to supply the demand. A competition carriage (c. £4,000) is precision-built for strength and speed, with disc brakes on all four wheels. In competition it carries four: the driver, the umpire and two grooms. Should a carriage turn over at speed, expert and urgent assistance is needed to sort out the tangle of legs, bodies and harness.

The team was put to the carriage. George climbed on to the box (driver's seat) and arranged the reins in his left hand. 'Stand Up!' — the horses' heads were free. 'Walk On!' 'Steady!' — they were keen to be off. We turned out of the stable yard, and 'Trot!' The horses are trained to work mainly to the spoken command. Down the back streets we went, to friendly greetings from passers-by. Under the echoing railway bridge and we were out on to a network of rough tracks that ramble between dry-stone walls.

'Trot on!' The horses slipped easily into an extended trot. One whistle put them into a canter. Two whistles would have had them going belly to the ground, and they wanted to go, but 'Steady now! Steady!' brought them back nicely in hand; George just gently feeling their mouths through the reins with his horseman's hands. Brute force would be no good: four horses would win every time. Had he ever been run away with? Oh yes: frightening and dangerous.

The track ran alongside the M6. Lorries, coaches and cars thundered by only a few feet away. The horses paid no attention. A grand bit for settling horses, said George. We seemed to be an unsettling sight for the occupants of a motor coach, who scrabbled to the windows as the coach flashed by. We clattered and jingled back through the edge of the town and crossed the A6. Then came a mile of hill that really brought the horses into their collars, whilst still keeping up the long, steady, distance-eating trot.

I asked George to explain the competition. Driving Trials happen over three days. The first day is Dressage: a series of movements at different paces to demonstrate handiness and exact control. Next day comes the Marathon; twenty-five kilometres in five stages. (A) A ten-km section at any pace, but the speed must average fifteen kph, neither more nor less; (B) a one-km walk at an average seven kph. Then there is a compulsory ten-minute halt and veterinary inspection. (C) A short, fast-trot section at an average eighteen kph; then (D) the same as (B). Another ten-minute halt follows, and the vet again, before the last section. (E) Ten kms with eight obstacles, which may include water and sharp turns on a steep bank; it must include a slalom of gates to be twisted through. On the third day there is Cone Driving in the ring. This is a timed competition that tests the suppleness of the horses; a cone knocked over is the equivalent of a rail down in show jumping.

We reached the top of the hill and met an amazing view across the Eden Valley to the distant Pennines. The sun was warm. The pleasant breeze brought wafts of baking hay. The

entle rhythm of our progress was very lulling. It was just the
moment for a rude shock. George brought the gently sweating
eam to a halt: 'Stand!' Then: 'Right, lad, you take 'em.' Me?
He could not mean me? But he was getting out of his seat and
anding me the reins, whilst the horses shook their heads
gainst the flies and stamped impatiently.

Thread the reins through the fingers of the left hand, drop
he right over the top of the reins for added purchase and
Walk on!' and 'Trot!' What an amazing sensation; to be
erched up there, looking down on those four surging, muscu-
ar, sinewy backs; to smell that marvellous brew of horse and
weat and leather. Most amazing of all, however, were the
ignals coming down the reins: the feeling of strength and
ower and suppressed speed. It was a heady draught, and
omplete duffer that I was, I knew that I was touching some-
hing very fine and very special. Why do people drive? Pick
p the reins of a team and you would not have to ask. I am
ery grateful to George Bowman for allowing me a small sip
rom his cup, but then everyone who knows him agrees that
e is not only the 'most consistent and successful carriage
river in Britain', but a lovely man as well. The strange thing
s that at the age of fifty-six he has just become allergic to
orses.

# Chapter Twenty-nine

# A HORSE CALLED NUNNINGTON

NUNNINGTON CAME FROM an Irish bog. Nunnington is a Household Cavalry 'Black Horse'. The millions of you who watched the Trooping the Colour at Her Majesty the Queen's Birthday Parade saw him doing his job. Nunnington and his rider, Captain Valentine de la Fargue Woyka, were immediately behind the second division of the Life Guards, and in front of the first division of the Blues and Royals (Royal Horse Guards and First Dragoons). Nunnington has not done badly for a boy from the bogs.

'Black Horse' is a generic term given to the troop horses of the Household Cavalry Mounted Regiment, for the very simple reason that they are all black, except for the trumpeters' horses (all greys), and the drum horses who can be any colour.

Every year the British Army buys between sixty and seventy horses. The majority still come from Eire. (It is worthy of note that after the IRA murder of horses and men in Hyde Park, six Black Horses were donated by the Irish people.) Besides the needs of the Household Cavalry, horses are required for the King's Troop (Royal Horse Artillery), the Royal Military Police, HQ – London District – and the Royal Army Veterinary Corps.

The RAVC runs the Defence Animal Centre at Melton Mowbray. The DAC is comprised of the Army Veterinary and Remount Centre, the Army School of Farriery and the Dog Training Centre for the Army and the RAF. The genial presiding genius at Melton is Lt. Colonel Peter Roffey, thirty-five years in the RAVC ('man and boy'), and a man in love with his work.

In the spring of 1986 Nunnington came to Melton as a wild, tousled, unbroken four-year-old. Although he had been vetted on purchase, he was vetted again, wormed and vaccinated. At that time he had no name: he was just Army Horse No. 7022. With the others of his intake he was turned out to grass under the care of Roy Kettle, the Estate Stable Manager. Throughout the summer, 7022 and his mates became accustomed to the halter and to having their feet trimmed regularly. This gets the young horses used to being handled, and to the noise and smell of the farrier's shop.

In the autumn, the young horses go to school. The Household Cavalry horses go to Windsor. The King's Troop school their young horses at Melton, which also retains twenty young horses for its own famous equitation courses. There are two courses every year: April to October for Other Ranks, and October to February for Officers. It is deemed meet and right that Officers should shiver through the winter; not that anyone is going to get cold around the Equitation Officer, Captain 'Sandy' Sanderson. Each member of the course has three horses: one unbroken, one half-trained, and one trained horse. By the end of the course, the unbroken horse must be half-trained, and the half-trained horse fully trained, or so help you. Four-and-a-half hours in the saddle is the daily norm.

'Elbows in, heels down! Look down!' Up down, up down. Bring your bloody legs back, you cavalry lads; like a lot of hunting farmers!' Up down, up down. 'Nice deep breath! Elbows in and your horse will walk; ride waaalk!'; for which relief and much thanks, I should think.

In October 1987, 7022 arrived at Combermere Barracks, Windsor to be 'broken'. The traditional methods involved long weeks of gentling, lungeing and long-reining before the moment of truth when a horse has a man on its back for the first time. This can be a traumatic experience for horse and man. Things can get broken. Corporal Major Pendry, the Warrant Officer in charge of training, can remember times when his face would be pitted and raw from 'buying some ground' in the cinder-surfaced breaking yard. Now the best of the traditional methods are being combined with those of Californian rancher, Monty Roberts. Mr Roberts has evolved a method of starting young horses by psychological methods. He can take any unbroken horse and be on its back, trotting, cantering and galloping within half-an-hour. Hard to believe? CM Pendry did not believe it either, until he saw it done and did it himself. Forty-three young horses have been started successfully by this method over the last two years; it can take two months off their training time.

As the young horses progress, they become accustomed to all the things they are likely to meet in their daily work. Armoured cars, road works and urban traffic become second nature.

It is at Windsor that young horses and young men meet for the first time. Household Cavalry recruits do their basic training at the Guards' Depot. They come to Windsor for sixteen weeks' 'khaki' riding instruction, before going to Knightsbridge for four weeks' training in the ceremonial kit. Most of them have never even touched a horse before they joined the Army. They may find it sore work and somewhat trying, but a notice on the door of the riding school says: 'Please leave your temper on the hook provided; it is not welcome in the riding school.' It is not all riding school and parade work. The Black Horse is expected to be versatile. Show jumping, eventing and hunter trialling are all officially deemed to be good education for horse and rider.

7022 came to Knightsbridge in 1988 and got his name. Troop horse names are like a roll of drums: Quiberon, Neustadt, Quatre Bras, Imperial. Each annual intake takes a different initial letter. In 1988 the letter was N. 7022 became Nunnington, after a village in Yorkshire. Nunnington and the Army got on well together. In the summer of 1989 Nunnington became part of the Musical Ride, and then did some continuation training at Melton. He was picked for promotion, being selected as a potential charger for the new Commanding Officer. Then came near disaster. On the journey back to London, Nunnington damaged his near-hind leg so badly that it took him a year to recover. It was then that Captain Woyka took him on. It should not be thought that the fact that Nunnington jumped beautifully and 'ran like a stag' in team chasing events had anything to do with the good Captain's choice.

come to know it. The Government Axe hangs over the Household Division.

I am quite prepared to admit to a lump in the throat as the Household Cavalry walked and then trotted past their Colonel-in-Chief. I know excellence when I see it, and there is a polished savagery about massed cavalry that makes the back of the neck tingle.

And what of Nunnington? You saw him gliding over Horseguards, his neck arched, his ears pricked; he was loving every minute of it.

It was after midnight when the Colonel, the Major and I paid our final visit to the stables. If we had dined well, then that was only in keeping with the standards set through the day. The Barracks were still, and the occasional lights still burning in the soldiers' quarters suggested that few others had stayed up late. The stables were quiet, with only the Night Guard, Trooper de Vere Walker, on his continuous round of the lines. The Black Horses lay in their stalls, or dozed on their feet. The only sound was the occasional rattle of a halter block, or the stamp of a hoof.

Nunnington was lying at ease in his box, but his ears were cocked and his eyes alert; the prospect of the odd sugar-lump may have helped. There was an air of peace and contentment as we wandered round savouring that special stable smell.

The Major spread his arms in an expansive gesture: 'They're lovely people, my Black Horses, just really lovely people.' Amen to that, and another sugar-lump to Nunnington.

## Chapter Thirty

# POISON, PROBLEMS AND GOOD INTENTIONS

M R RON DAVIES is the Junior Agriculture Spokesman for the Labour Party. He has recently conducted a 'fundamental review' of country sports. He has concluded that the killing of foxes by hounds (where death is instantaneous) is cruel. He and his 'scientists and representatives of rural interests' have decided that poison gas is the best method. Now the convenient thing about gassing is that whatever happens, happens below ground in the fox's earth; 'what the eye don't see, the heart don't fret about'. I beg leave to doubt whether Mr Davies and his 'scientists' have ever seen the results of poison gas. I have. The next bit is not nice.

Bert was (and is) a keen hunter and lover of foxes. Every year there was a litter of cubs in a small earth on his farm, which fact gave him much delight. He telephoned me one morning in great distress. The evening before he had watched the cubs playing round the earth. That morning the earth was still and the holes blocked. The earth had been gassed. He asked me to investigate. We went up with spades and very carefully began to open the earth. Care was necessary because cyanide gas is very nasty stuff. It is also illegal to use this particular gas for foxes.

It was only a small earth. The cubs were in a huddled heap at the back of the den. The vixen had come forward in the tube to guard her babes against the unseen and deadly intruder. Her lips were drawn back in a rictus. Bright green slime and froth had filled her mouth and had dribbled on to the ground around her. The whole family had died hard and horribly. I have never forgotten the sight. My experience suggests that

Mr Ron Davies's conclusions are flawed; never mind the animals, let's bash the toffee-nosed hunters: the Politics of Poison all round.

One of the pleasures of my life is the Big Wood in the early morning. I am usually there in the grey of the dawn. At this time of year, the wood is full of birdsong. Every Scots Pine seems to be topped by a thrush singing its heart out.

I never saw the old doe, but she must have winded me, and away she went barking her alarm call. Some time later I had worked my way into a stand of mature pines and had become part of a tree. Four trees away, a red squirrel was being very acrobatic. He kept me entertained until another movement in some birch scrub caught the eye. The quietly grazing roe buck was a good one. I had seen him before and had decided to leave him.

The rocky knowe gives a good view of the space that has been clear felled. I spent an hour sitting under a boulder watching four does well in kid feeding quietly below me. By now the sun was warm and I had been up for five hours. Hat over the eyes and a little doze perhaps? But no, it was time to go home and start work. Still, there was breakfast to look forward to: definitely a two-egg day.

I suppose that Bureaucrats must be numbered amongst my pet (and petty) hates. I am filled with horror at the thought of having yet another legion of these pests let loose on us after our lemming-like plunge into Europe. I certainly never voted for that. We have quite enough home-bred ones, thank you very much.

My definitive Bureaucrat is the man to whom I confided that I was looking forward to a week of holiday in Spain (my only holiday).

'Ho!' he said. 'It's all right for some. Can't see me getting a holiday this year.'

'But I thought you chaps all got six weeks?'

He drew himself up in an offended manner. 'That's leave,' he said, 'that's not a holiday.'

Chapter Thirty-one

# HOUNDS ACROSS THE BORDER

Parts of the valley road are still sheet ice. The sensible motorcyclist wheels delicately. The road twists for miles between the rocky river and the sweeping hillsides. The tarmac just manages to last as far as Duncan's house, where it gives a sigh of relief and hands over to ancient, rutted tracks that wind upwards through the heather and bents.

Duncan and his dogs are just coming in off the hill when I arrive. We agree that it is 'gey card', but 'Man, what a day'. As indeed it is. The sun is already climbing into a cloudless sky. There is no wind, but the icy air reams out the lungs. Such golden days are rare in the Cheviots at the end of January. Little black Trixie the terrier comes scuttling and squeaking from her kennel and leaps with practised ease on to Duncan's petrol tank. She is tucked away in her travelling position, down the front of his jacket, with just her head sticking out. Then we are all ready: two men, two shepherd's bikes and Trixie; we are going to the Hounds.

Generations of feet, wheels and hooves must have carved out the old green roads over the Border. The tracks are obvious in places, but then disappear amongst banks of lying snow, rushes and bog slime. This is Duncan's patch, and I faithfully follow his broad back as we bump, wallow and thump our way always outwards and upwards.

We come to a wicket in a long wire fence that stretches out of sight in either direction. This is the 'Scotch Fence' – the Border. The sun is warm on the back now, and even at this height there is no wind and not a cloud in the ice-blue sky. But the view: man, what a view: those hills to the north, with the white tails of snow still on them, will be a good fifty miles away.

The country to the north of the fence is more dramatic, dropping away in great heather and boulder-strewn clefts. The sheep lie drier and more sheltered here than on the English side, and these are famous stock farms. The Gate is one of these farms, and today's meeting place. There is a large gathering. The local farming community is there on foot, horse and shepherding bikes. There are even a couple of visiting redcoats amongst the mounted field. Border hospitality flows freely amongst them all.

But the hounds are away! There is a rush to return glasses and thank the hosts. Hounds are already spread like a flock of gulls on the opposite hillside, their wonderful noses searching for a taint of fox. There is a small larch plantation at the bottom of the valley, and from it comes a great shout of hound voices. There are two, no, three, foxes in the spinney, and hounds are soon split in three different lots on the steep sides of the huge natural basin. There is nothing for the watchers to do but get themselves to a vantage point and wait.

A line of hounds disappears over the opposite hill and into the next valley, accompanied by two toy-like mounted figures. Five hundred feet below us a fox comes picking his way quietly across the scree face. Half-a-mile along the hillside a handful of hounds are struggling on his scent. From the top end of the basin a matchstick figure begins to semaphore violently. A horseman comes galloping back. Most of the hounds have slipped away at the top end, and are away through the 'English Fence'. The ground we cross is 'rough, a bit': peat bogs where a horse may sink to its belly; great, rough, tussocky 'bull snouts' and snow banks of unknown depth.

Twenty minutes of bad going brings us to the edge of a sweeping valley on the English watershed. All is silent and still, the sheep undisturbed all around. Time to sit in the heather in the sun and open the 'bait tin'. On the farthest hill the sheep start to bunch. A faint hound voice comes on the still air, and there they are, fast-moving distant dots, 'coming in' over the rolling hill about two miles away.

Pointing fingers and a quiver of excitement, and there is the run fox loping steadily down the burn far below and heading for the green fastness of conifers at the valley foot. The better going of the lower slopes lets us push on a bit, but the pack is flying now. They are in the trees by the time we arrive on the opposite hill; the cry swells and takes on a special edge. The end comes quickly and cleanly in the burn at the bottom of the trees. 'He was a guid fox,' says a bearded shepherd. 'Aye,' says his companion, 'but he's one less for the lambing time.'

Chapter Thirty-two

# THE CLEAN BOOT

THE SWEATING MAN struggles across the open down; the big black hounds close on him inexorably, their deep, triumphant baying mingling with the cruel urging of voice and horn from the red-coated huntsman. Surely this must be the ultimate 'Blood Sport'? Surely this must be the moment for you to hide your horrified face in your trembling hands? Well, no, not really; you may open your eyes and read on without a qualm.

Hunting 'The Clean Boot' is the hunting of a running man (or woman) with hounds. Hounds hunt the natural body scent of the runner. The hound most favoured for the Clean Boot is the cross-bred bloodhound. The pure-bred bloodhound has suffered much from show-bench-induced in-breeding. A judicious dash of foxhound blood is required to restore stamina and working abilities.

There are currently four bloodhound packs operating in England. 'It is quite different to foxhunting,' says Major William Stringer, the leading expert on the Clean Boot. Major Stringer started the Weser Vale Bloodhounds when he was serving in Germany with the Blues and Royals. In 1971 he was posted back to Windsor, and founded the Windsor Forest Bloodhounds. He is now the Hunt Chairman, and was on parade at Burrow Farm, Hambleden, where Mr and Mrs David Palmer hosted a recent meet of the Windsor Forest. Foxhunting needs a lot of space. It certainly might have its problems in the pretty, but cramped, countryside between Marlow and Henley. It is in this sort of area that Boot hunting comes into its own.

The Master of the WFB in 1991 was Mrs Ruth Coyne, an

Irish lady of great charm and determination. She needed both at Burrow Farm, as she was hobbling about with a broken leg in plaster. Her beloved hounds were to be hunted for the first time by the whipper-in, Ian Smeeth, who had only been with them a week. He brought eight couple of big, black-and-tan, floppy-eared, wrinkly-faced hounds to the 12.30 p.m. meet. Most of them, very sensibly, curled up and went to sleep, whilst the hot punch and politeness were handed round. There were some twenty-five mounted followers, and a large crowd of enthusiasts on foot.

Quarry for the day was David Jefferies, a well-known cross-country runner from Maidenhead. At 1.00 p.m. he set off down the combe below the farm, leaving a singlet from which the hounds could fill their noses. It might lead to unhappiness if they hunted the wrong person. It is possible to vary the pace of a hunt according to the amount of 'law' given to the runner. The Major favours thirty to forty-five minutes. This makes the hunt last longer, and makes for more interesting hound work. Only about fifteen minutes' law was given this time. Hounds picked up the scent from the vest, and went booming away. We all piled into a Land-Rover and drove furiously to head off the runner. Hounds were too fast and had already caught David, who looked very well on it, when we got there.

Three lines per day are the norm. The WFB favour hunts of about three miles. Burrow Farm is liberally sprinkled with nice little post-and-rails. We set off in good time to get to the end of the second line. The photographer was desperate for blood and gore. As we waited in a field we could hear the deep, tuba- and bassoon-like voices of the hounds getting closer and closer. A sweating figure came into sight, still going well. The great, dark hounds came roaring into view and overhauled their hapless victim in the middle of the field. No gruesome scenes, I fear; not unless you class having a hand licked by a large pink tongue as Adults Only Viewing.

For the last line we established ourselves by a bridge in the picturesque Hambleden Vale. Here there is a nasty 'in and out' across a lane. There our *schadenfreude* might be gratified by a fall or two. We could see the runner coming for a good distance, battling his way through hordes of hikers going the other way. Might there be problems here? The camera man licked his lips.

Hounds hunted fast and hard up the valley, ignoring the Great Bobble-Hatted. The mounted followers were pounding on a field behind. Hounds 'killed' by the churchyard, and all the riders jumped in and out of the lane too beautifully.

So that was that: everybody well-galloped and happy by 3.00 p.m., and nothing more to do but take a bun and a glass of whisky out of William Kaye's hospitable Range-Rover. It is impossible to compare the Clean Boot with foxhunting. It would be like comparing vintage port to lager beer; both are excellent at the right time and in the right place. There is no doubt that the Windsor Forest Bloodhounds succeed excellently, and are entirely right for their time and place.

# Chapter Thirty-three

# IN WHICH POLITICS AND FINGERS MAY BOTH BE GRUBBY

THERE IS NOTHING like starting with a few statistics. It is estimated that 2,500 miles of hedge get grubbed out each year in England and Wales. It is estimated that the aboriginal rural population represents *c.* two per cent of the voting population (and falling).

There are still some 300,000 miles of surviving hedges in England and Wales, and there is an encouraging amount of new planting. This seems to put the hedges in a better position than those who live and work amongst them. There are some very ancient hedges. Some of the parish boundary hedges are supposed to date back to Saxon times. The vast majority of these hedges are less than 200 years old. For centuries before that a great deal of England was open common land. The rights to make use of common land usually went with the hearthstone of a village house. The house might tumble down, but as long as the hearthstone maintained, then so did the rights. I once had the rights to six 'sheep gaits' on a Yorkshire common.

Common Rights might vary, but they usually included the right to graze cows, sheep, pigs or geese; to collect dead wood, cut furze, or dig peat for fuel. The Rights were of very ancient origin, and were vital to the survival of the English peasant economy. The commoners did not own the commons. They actually belonged to the Lord of the Manor. He could do what he liked with them, provided that he did not disturb the rights of the commons. So, if the commoners had grazing rights, the Lord could not disturb those rights by ploughing up the common, or digging for coal, or whatever.

The late eighteenth and early nineteenth centuries brought great advances in agriculture and industry. The landowners began to look longingly on the 'wastes'. Could not these inefficient pieces of land be improved to produce more food and minerals for the general good? And if the owners did well by doing good, then so much the better. As for the peasants, more productive labour could be found for them in a 'dark satanic mill'; thereby 'improving' them as well. So the Enclosure Acts enabled the commons to be enclosed with nice new hedges and improved to the greater good. 'The law will punish man or woman, who steals a goose from off the Common; but lets the greater felon loose who steals the Common from the goose.' The Enclosure Acts did for the English peasant as surely as the Highland Clearances did for the Scottish clansman.

A trip to France will be helpful in understanding the political legacy of the enclosure of the commons. In France, the peasant (*'peasant'* is perfectly respectable usage in France) is alive and well and politically kicking. The extended family of aunts, uncles and cousins are all likely to have a financial and emotional stake in the family holding, and be passionate in its defence. The French rural vote is reckoned to be *c.* thirty-seven per cent, and when the peasants sneeze the Government comes galloping with a box of tissues and something for the Financial *Grippe*.

As far as British politicians are concerned we 'Two Per Cent Peasants' are a minor irritant which can safely be ignored in electoral terms; our traditional way of life can be grubbed up like a hedge. It is partly our own fault. We ignored the lessons of history, and 'put our trust in princes'. We listened to the politicians when they told us to be fruitful and multiply. 'Invest in your farms,' they said. 'Increase your productivity: your country needs you,' they said. So we did. We invested and borrowed money to improve our farms. British farmers became the most efficient and productive in Europe. Then came the rise of Green Fascism. The politicians fell over each other to get in behind. The countryman is now a public enemy; his traditional sports are to be suppressed, and his home and livelihood are in jeopardy.

The Two Per Cent Peasants are pretty much in the same situation as the Sioux Indians were. The politicians have spoken with forked tongue, and the 'White Settlers' want to get rid of us and take our land. When we replay the 'Little Bighorn', I shall play the part of Crazy Horse and, whilst I am stropping my scalping knife, perhaps you would like to propose a suitable politician for the Custer role.

Food Hygiene is something that concerns people mightily these days. Many people will not eat anything that has not been packaged to the point of total impenetrability. Has anyone calculated the amount of resources wasted on useless packaging? It is possible that country people have a more robust approach than their urban brethren. The brown paper bag, or a couple of sheets of the *Blankshire Advertiser*, will still suffice. A bit of honest dirt adds flavour.

'You'll eat a peck of dirt before you die,' says the Goodwife as she picks the sausages off the floor. She is not going to have any frivolous complaints about bits of fluff and grit. ''Twill all come off in the flour,' says the lady who has brought her hands straight from the stable to the mixing bowl. Her pastry is so delicious that no one is going to worry if it is a bit grey: must be highly organic.

The two ramblers obviously enjoyed refreshing themselves from a cool clear hill stream. It is good to partake of Nature's bounty. They remarked on the excellence of the water, so different to the chemical-flavoured stuff that comes out of the tap. It would have done them no good to tell them that they had been half a mile downstream from the run-off of Bert's septic tank: 'What the eye don't see, the heart don't fret about'.

cough, and away to the forest for more deer watching. Then it was back to the larder for 'skinning and basic jointing', which puts one in splendid fettle for an enormous breakfast. The rest of the day was devoted to the Rifle Range and the Simulated Stalk. Part of the forest had been dotted with life-size cut-outs of deer of different types, ages and species; some easy to spot, some difficult. The student, accompanied by a ranger, had to stalk as for real and decide whether each particular deer was possible to shoot (clear shot to vital organs), safe to shoot (against a slope), correct to shoot (in season), and suitable to shoot (age and condition). All the time the guide told him what he had done wrong, or even right. John Cubby, with his knowledge and his dry wit, is a wonderful stalking companion. At the end, he shook my hand and said that 'for a slim little chap you haven't stalked bad'. I felt as if I had won a prize.

The Grizedale course was superbly organized, and of such educational value that I will even forgive BASC that ghastly night in the bothy.

Chapter Thirty-five

# OF DOES AND FOOLS AND DOUBLE-BREASTED GUNS

A T ABOUT 5 O'CLOCK this morning I was on the mooch up the side of straggly thorn hedge. On my left the ground sloped upwards: a big new grass ley. On the other side of the hedge was a rough, boggy corner of grass and rushes. The Squire has dug a pond there, and it was raucous with black-headed gulls and a piping pair of oyster catchers. I was on the look-out for an old roe buck who is reputed to lie up there. He has never been there when I have, and he was not there again today. So I was leaning on my stick watching the early sunlight on the eastern slopes of the Cheviots, wondering whether I should carry on and try to stalk the rough bit by the river; or should I go home and have some breakfast? It was a bitingly cold east wind, and my foot was hurting and . . . and then I happened to glance up the big field on the left-hand side. There was a lovely big roe doe standing on the skyline. She must have just come over the crest. She had not seen me, which is not surprising, because I look pretty much like a blackthorn bush even when I am wearing my Town Suit.

The doe was quite at ease, looking about her. All of a sudden a hare jumped up just in front of her and came flat out down the field towards me. The doe jumped and then took off after the hare, belly to ground. She was chasing the hare just for the fun of it. I have no doubt about this, because if the hare turned so did the doe, and when the hare eventually jinked through a hedge, the doe flew it in pursuit. Then she suddenly tired of her game and popped back over the wire and stopped for a blow. She was less than twenty feet away

from me. I kept very, very, still, and she did not see me. She
just stood there whiffling her nose and flicking her ears. Then
she must have got a rank whiff of human. She was gone like a
bullet from a stand to a full gallop. What wonderful movers
deer are; which is more than could be said for me, as I hobbled
back up the hill to the van.


The suggestion from the Police Federation that all those who
shoot game should pass some sort of test has produced some
fairly predictable huffing and puffing from the Double-Barrelled
Brotherhood. I suppose that I ought to be bristling a bit as
well, but I do not think that it is a bad idea. As I understand
the suggestion, the test would cover not only some basic
safety drill ('suppose you dropped your shotgun and got some
snow in the barrels; would you still fire it?' Well, would you?),
but also some basic knowledge about the quarry species and
the countryside. Some fairly nasty things have been emerging
from the game shooters' woodshed lately. These unacceptable
practices have their roots in ignorance and greed. As things
stand, any untrained fool can buy a gun and a pheasant shoot
in the same afternoon, and cause havoc and devastation at his
leisure. This is bad for shooting and bad for rural life as a
whole.

A little basic training is never a bad thing, and the more I
think about it, the more I think that the principle might be
expanded. Let us test the shooters by all means, but why
should we not extend the basic idea so that all those who visit
the countryside should be tested and licensed? We hear a lot
about the environmental damage caused by an ever-increasing
flood of visitors to the countryside. Many of these problems
are caused by ignorance. Let there be a Certificate of Rural
Competence (CRUC). Those who fail the test would not be
allowed to stray beyond motorway service areas.

Now I suppose that some of you will take the hump and
say that if that is Poole's attitude then we will not let the
blighter into London without a City of London Orienteering
Test (CLOT). Can he find his way from Heathrow to the Isle
of Dogs via Pudding Lane on Public Transport? Almost

certainly not. However, I have now discovered the definitive method of getting across London. Travel in a car with a certain badge on it and the strait is made broad, the rough smooth; red lights are meaningless; the Constabulary holds back the traffic at every junction, and you can drive straight across Hyde Park Corner (wherever that is). I recommend it as a thoroughly efficient method of transport, and you do not need to know your Piccadilly from your Bakerloo.

Chapter Thirty-six

# WEAVING A STORY

HARRIS TWEED IS a unique cloth. Its uniqueness has been legally defined by the full majesty of the Scottish courts: 'Harris Tweed must be made from Scottish wool, dyed, one hundred per cent spun and finished in the Outer Hebrides and hand-woven by the islanders at their homes in the islands of Lewis, Harris, Uist, Barra and their several purtenances.'

I have worn and loved Harris Tweed for years. It lasts for years. Indeed, much of my Harris Tweed was inherited, and I still relish its rugged hairiness and the heather and peat smoke smell it gives off when wet. The cloth was originally made to keep at bay the full rigours of the Hebridean climate. The smell came from the dyes made of roots, lichens and herbs. In 1840 Lady Dunmore started taking the cloth to London and selling it to her friends on behalf of the crofters. Harris Tweed had arrived in Society. But how does this wonderful cloth maintain in these days of garish, sweaty 'lons and 'lenes?

Stornoway is the capital of the Outer Hebrides, and the home of the Harris Tweed Association. The presiding genial genius is Callum MaCauley, for whose patience, time and help I am very grateful. Without Callum's help I would have got nowhere. Lewis is an independent, tightly woven, Gaelic-speaking community. English journalists are not always regarded as bargain of the week.

Ian MacKenzie is thirty-eight, and was taught to weave by his father. Like many of the 400 self-employed weavers, Ian is a crofter. None of the ones that I met would actually admit to liking weaving, but 'you can weave when you want to'; so if you are busy at the sheep during the day, then you can weave all night. Also 'it pays the bills'. A ninety-metre roll of cloth takes about ten hours to weave, and brings the weaver £80-100.

Ian introduced me to the Hattersley Domestic Loom. This is the almost universal loom used by the weavers. Ian's machine is eighty years old, and still weaving strong. Hattersley Domestics usually lurk in a special shed behind the croft. They are amazingly Heath Robinsonesque — cast-iron machines with whirring wheels, flying shuttles and metal arms that jerk and clank. The power is pedal, and the noise is such as to prohibit conversation. But they work. For two years Ian has been testing a prototype of a new loom: the Bonas Griffith Intermediate Technology Loom, which is smaller, lighter, quieter and quicker. It will also weave double-width cloth, which is now the world standard. Harris Tweed's current limitation to single-width (*c.* thirty inches) production seems to be a problem; potential buyers love the quality, but not the width.

Derek Murray is the third generation of his family to own and run Kenneth Macleod (Shawbost) Ltd, one of the two main mills on the island. He explained the workings of tweed making. The wool is bought at the Edinburgh auctions, already washed and scoured. The blending, dyeing (all chemical now, and no smell), carding and spinning is all done at the mill by sophisticated modern machinery. The warping of the spun yarn is still done by hand on a frame of wooden pegs; a vital and highly skilled job (warp is the longitudinal thread of a piece of cloth, across which the weft yarn is woven). Warp, weft and design instructions are then sent to a weaver. They are usually dumped in bags at the croft gate, where the rolls of woven tweed are waiting. Back at the mill the raw tweed is washed, milled and pressed in huge mangles. Then every inch is checked and tidied up by ladies with sharp eyes and scissors. The finished tweed is stamped and packed ready for shipment to Germany, France, Canada, Australia and even Leeds. Mention the USA to the Harris Tweed Men and they become pensive. For a long time the American market absorbed over forty per cent of the cloth's output, but now the fickle fashion market has turned away.

Harris Tweed is fighting back.

Robin Huggan is the designer for Kenneth MacKenzie Ltd,

the other big mill on Lewis. He produces over one hundred ranges of colour and design each year: different designs for different countries. It really is 'export or die' for Harris Tweed. To meet modern demand there are now lightweight (eight/nine ozs) and featherweight (six/seven ozs) tweeds. The redoubtable Bruce Burns, who has come out of retirement to resuscitate a bankrupt mill, is producing a 'gossamer weight' to do battle on the Paris market.

Harris Tweed is smart and comfortable. Its provenance gives the cloth an unassailable 'environmental credibility'. 'What we need,' said Callum, 'is for some famous person to start wearing Harris Tweed and set a new fashion trend.' I did point out that I had been wearing it for years, but he just gave me a polite, sad smile in Gaelic.

Chapter Thirty-seven

# KIPPERS AND CORBIE CROWS

O N MY RECENT visit to the Isle of Lewis, I rubbed my hands and, perhaps, salivated a little at the prospect of breakfasting off a 'Stornoway Kipper'. The wretched thing arrived over-cooked and about the size of a large butterfly. That poor little herring should never have been caught, let alone kippered. It seems that our fishing industry is in a poor way, with too many boats chasing too few fish. Many areas are fished out.

This unhappy state can be blamed on the EC and successive British governments, who have neglected the interests of our fishermen. The Common Fisheries Policy says that all community fishermen shall have common access to community fishing grounds. All very nice and fair you might think, except for the fact that most of the fish were in British waters. 'Were' is the important word. Since all the foreign boats came whooping and hollering into fishing grounds from which they had been excluded, there are precious few fish left. All the little herring that should have been allowed to grow up and become great, juicy kippers are being scooped up and made into fishmeal. Fishmeal is used to grow crops and animals that nobody wants to buy.

The British fishermen are not very happy about this rape of their stock. They are even less happy about the EC directive that keeps their boats tied up in port for eight consecutive days in each month. This directive (largely ignored by other nations anyway) may look fine in the oily calm of Brussels. It looks different in the treacherous waters of the Minch, especially if the weather knocks another week or two out of the working month. There is a very real worry that desperation may drive men to fish in unsuitable weather, of which the Outer Hebrides has a plentiful supply.

So the Scottish fishermen are depressed in spirit and pocket. No doubt but they have been greatly cheered by that Nice Mr Gummer. He announced that the eight-day tie-up would help them with their Sabbath observance. I talked to one of Mr Gummer's constituents the other day; he said: 'John's a nice chap, but the trouble is that he thinks that all his utterances come straight from God.' I wonder whether British farmers and fishermen really deserve the Ministrations of such a saintly man.

I suppose the answer to the more ludicrous EC directives is to do what the Continentals do: pretend to agree with them and then just ignore them. There is a valuable lesson in Eurothink there.

There was a recent EC move to put carrion crows and magpies on a protected list. I drove past a field the other day and counted fourteen magpies hopping about. There will be precious few little hedgerow birds who will manage to raise broods in that area: magpies are consummate nest robbers.

This is the time of year when my game hens produce their chicks. The game fowl live a semi-wild existence around the yard and the sheep shed. They are experts at concealing themselves and their nests. The next thing you know is that there is a clucking hen in the yard surrounded by a cheeping brood of tiny puffballs. All very nice too: I like to see plenty of broods about the place. So do the corbies (carrion crows). There is one hard-bitten old villain in particular who has taken to haunting the yard. Any chick that strays from the anxious mother is not likely to have a second chance. He is very wily, this old sinner. I nearly had him stalked the other night. Up went the shotgun: up drove Patricia and away went the corbie.

'Good,' said Patricia, 'you shouldn't shoot such lovely creatures.'

What about the chicks, the eggs and the weakly lamb, with its eyes and tongue pecked out whilst it was still alive?

'Oh well, I didn't know they did that sort of thing. I hope you shoot him next time,' she said. So do I, and if the EC brings in some barmy nonsense about crows and magpies then I shall approach the problem in the proper European Spirit.

In the last couple of years, I have planted a five-acre wood at the top of the farm, and another five-acre wood with a pond at the bottom. The top wood has a resident barn owl, who now has two palatial nesting boxes at his/her disposal. The pond area has a resident kestrel. The other day the owl strayed down to the pond. The kestrel thought this to be right out of order. I watched an aerial combat with some superb flying on both sides. In the end the owl conceded and went home. I would dearly love to see them both breed on the farm.

# Chapter Thirty-eight

# TREES, TRUSTS AND WILLIAM-THE-CONQUEROR

FIVE THOUSAND YEARS ago sixty per cent of Great Britain was covered by indigenous woodland. Over the centuries much of this woodland has been systematically destroyed. Timber was needed for ship-building and iron-smelting. Much land has been cleared for agriculture, but before you start a bout of righteous indignation about the wicked farmers, just think of all the trees that have been destroyed for urban development and new roads. For all these reasons, indigenous woodland today covers only three per cent of Britain, and much of it is derelict or going that way.

On the credit side of the environmental ledger, there has been a significant planting of small woodlands during the last 150 years. These are the copses that help to make up the much clichéd 'patchwork quilt' of the countryside. Most of these small woodlands were planted for the express purpose of providing homes for foxes and pheasants. They also provide a habitat for many animals, birds and plants.

Proper woodland management is expensive, and many woodlands have become run-down. High capital taxation has also meant that many woods have been placed on the market, and all too often have disappeared under the developers' bulldozers. To halt this decline a group of concerned environmentalists got together and founded the Badminton Conservation Trust. It was so named in memory of that great naturalist, the late Duke of Beaufort. The objects of the Trust are . . .

to manage and maintain woodlands for the benefit of

future generations; to ensure re-planting and natural re-generation of indigenous species; to protect national fauna and flora in the woodland environment, respecting sporting rights and interests; to make the woodland accessible to young people for instructive, supervised study.

Peakes Covert is typical of the small woodlands that are coming under the Trust's protection. In 1868 Colonel Peake returned from India to live at Burrough Hall in Leicestershire. In the sheltered valley below his house, he planted a seven-and-a-half-acre fox covert. Peakes Covert maintains to this day, albeit in a somewhat tattered state. It has recently been acquired by the Badminton Trust.

I visited the covert with the Trust Chairman, Lady Hastings, two well-known local naturalists — Brian Fanshawe and Clem Adkins — and fifty-six children of the Langham C. of E. Primary School with their Headmistress, Mrs Maggie Wilson. We strode across the wolds in a straggle of bright anoraks and cheerful chatter. The half-eaten remains of a lamb provoked a great deal of interest and a discussion on foxes and their habits.

Much of the north end of the covert had been a derelict waste of bramble and elder bushes. The rubbish has been cleared and replanted with thorn, as it had been originally. After about twelve years of growth the thorn will be 'cut and laid' (the stems cut partly through and laid over, so that the thorn continues to grow). This makes a snug and effective shelter for many forms of wild life, and is vandal-proof. At the south end there had been a straggling coppice of ash and sycamore, which the Woodland Consultant had deemed value-less. This too had been cut and laid. The new coppice growth springing from it will eventually get the same treatment, making a living stick-heap.

The children took a lively interest in what they saw. They were full of questions about birds and plants. There were also more technical problems. 'How many miles is an acre?' asked my new friend William-the-Conqueror. I passed the buck to Peter Nelmes, the Deputy Head. There was a certain comfort in finding that the metric/imperial bog made him flounder a bit too.

On the bank beside the covert we inspected a fox's breeding earth, and then a huge badger sett at the top of the bank. Brian Fanshawe tramped manfully through a patch of gorse to see if he could disturb a fox for us to see. The whins were blank, to everyone's disappointment. However, the badgers' latrine caused great interest. Richard found some sheep's vertebrae which he was going to turn into a sculpture back at school, and William-the-Conqueror found a badger's skull: all very educational. It had been interesting to see the two prongs of the Badminton Trust's fork: the preservation of an important piece of wildlife habitat, and the interest and enthusiasm of the children for the future of the countryside. The Trust seems a good way forward. I am now a member.

# Chapter Thirty-nine

# SPRING, *SHEEP SENSE AND* POLITICAL STUPIDITY

THIS IS THE best growing time that I can remember for several years. The winter snows have topped up the springs that ran dry during the recent Mediterranean summers. The spring rains came late and have stayed late. This time last year the tops of the hills that I can see from the office window were already starting to 'burn off' and turn brown with drought. This year everything is green and lush. The hayfield down by the village looks positively luxuriant, and has been a mass of wild flowers.

In my little wood at the top of my farm, the newly planted trees struggled through two baking summers. At best they survived; many died. In this damp spring, they have taken off with a whoop and a holloa; the growth has been amazing. The fenced-off plantation has produced an increase in wild life. There are partridges nesting, as well as the resident barn owl. He/she can often be seen perched on one of the plastic tree tubes that protect the young trees from rabbits and hares. 'Hares are rare' cry the naturalists: up here they are not; I counted twelve in one field the other morning.

It was also three years since we dug that pond at the bottom of the farm. The pond never became much more than a mud-pan during the dry years, so this year it was dug deeper. Now it is truly a pond with two islands. A pair of oyster catchers have been showing an interest in leasing one of them. And we have tadpoles, masses and masses of tadpoles.

One of the most attractive features of the pond are the Welly Boots. I was inspecting the freshly dug spoil, one cold, wet, late-winter morning, when I found myself sinking. I got one boot half out, which drove the other one deeper into the sludge. I struggled and slurped and glugged, sinking deeper all the time, watched with fascinated interest by the collies, who thought that it must be some splendid new game. At last the sludge reached the top of the boots and there was only one thing for it: Abandon Boots. A half-mile walk through wintry mud in stockinged feet concentrates the mind wonderfully. The boots are still there, entombed with just their tops showing. I suppose that I could plant something in them.

I have mentioned my game fowl, who live a semi-wild life in and around the sheep shed. The other morning there was a frightful noise and kerfuffle outside my bedroom window. I leaped from my bed and there was an old vixen with a hen in her mouth. She was within six feet of the house. I opened the window and reasoned with her in a Christian Spirit. She cocked her wicked old eye at me and trotted sedately off down the field with her breakfast. She has had at least ten hens since, but worst of all she has had Ginger, the Black-Breasted Light Red stud cock. Ginger feared nothing on two legs or four. But it may be that the loss of an eye, in one of his fratricidal struggles for the supremacy of the dung heap, may have been his undoing. There is an irony here. Throughout the twenty-five years that I was a Master of Foxhounds, no fox ever came near my fowl. Like everybody else, the foxes obviously feel that I am now a person of no consequence. Mind you, I saw the old girl's family the other day – three strapping cubs. I cannot begrudge her the odd hen, but she might have left Ginger.

We shepherds call it 'mothering-up'; the Caring Professions call it 'maternal bonding'. It is the same thing. We want the baby to love its mummy and vice versa. In the ovine world the bond is usually straightforward; there are always a few problem-mothers, however, who try to kick their offspring out of the pen, or give them a good head-butting. It is possible that there are some human mummies who are not too keen on baby to start off with. I have no doubt but that the

Caring Professions have skilled psychologists in their ranks who deal with this sort of thing. We also use psychology: it is called the 'what-the-eye-don't-see-the-heart-don't-fret-about syndrome'. The old bisom's neck is clamped in a yoke, thus enabling the lambs to suckle unmolested. The ewe stays there until her maternal instincts have rallied a bit.

We then allow the bonding to set, by keeping the ewes and lambs in small groups. This makes mum easy to find when you have been dozing in the sun and wake with a horrid start to find a collie dog sniffing you. Each group is passed through a series of pens and fields, the group gradually increasing in size. By the end of a week the bonding should be firm.

One of the pleasant jobs on a fine May evening is wandering round with dog and stick, making sure that all is well and that all the lambs get their bedtime milk. I can produce a particularly piercing whistle between my front teeth: this is the 'mother-up' whistle. The dog snakes away round the edge of the field. The ewes know that that whistle means 'dog coming'. The field immediately becomes a mass of trotting mothers blaring for their offspring. The lambs drop whatever they are doing (like playing tag down the hedge back) and race bleating to find mother. On reaching home-base, they immediately dive under the skirts of the fleece and tuck-in. What I want to see is two little tails wagging enthusiastically from under each ewe. This is 'mothering-up'.

The thing that always fascinates me is how lambs will dash unerringly through one hundred ewes to find their own mother. Now I know that any human mother could pick out her lamb from all the other squalling bundles in the hospital. She would recognize it instantly by sight, of course, quite apart from the fact that it has a large label on its toe saying 'Baby Harrison'. With sheep it is obvious that the voice is the primary method of contact. The lambs recognize their mother's blare out of all the others. Next comes smell. Mutual sniffing confirms the contact and only then will the lambs dive in. I know that it is all perfectly natural and straightforward, but, like most things in nature, it is still a little miracle, and I still wonder at it afresh each year.

# Chapter Forty

# A BOARING MATTER

'HAPPY AS A BOAR in straw' seems a good way to describe Chris Pinder. Chris farms 'wild boars': they are not wild, and they are obviously not all boars, but that is the official MAFF description, like it or lump it. MAFF also classifies the wild boar as a 'dangerous animal'. In fact the wild pig is shy and retiring, but as far as the Ministry is concerned, Chris is not a farmer but a zoo keeper, and has to be licensed as such.

Chris was a heavy-plant man, following pipelines and motorways all over Britain. Farming is in his blood, and wherever his heavy plant has rumbled, he has tried to have a base where he could keep a few animals. He wanted an outdoor pig for his smallholding. At the Rare Breeds Sale at Edinburgh a wild boar sow (blatant sexism) came through the ring and went cheap because 'nobody knew what it was'.

Two years ago he left the contracting life and set up Wilbore Farm on five acres of windswept hillside in Co Durham. Wilbore Farm today is a collection of sheds and caravans. All the building has been done by Chris. He also plans to build his own house.

There is a good welcome in the yard at Wilbore: Poppy, the Alsatian, gives the visitor a good sniffing; Manx Loghtan lambs rub against your legs, and a scampering mass of striped piglets appear from every corner and play a squeaking, grunting game of ring of roses. All the while Chris grins happily through his flaming-red beard.

At present there are two boars and fourteen sows on the farm, plus some one hundred 'growers' of various ages. The sows can be managed so as to produce two litters per year, and the farm sells some 200 pigs per annum. The wild boar growers take twelve months to reach the killing stage, as against the fourteen weeks for 'battery pigs'. Wild pigs cannot be 'forced'. They are very susceptible to stress, and so they have to live as natural a life as possible if they are to thrive. They are not castrated, de-tailed, or de-tusked. The sows wallow happily in large outdoor pens, with snug, dry huts to retire into. They are brought into the buildings to farrow and then go out again. As long as they are suckling, the little striped piglets run wild about the place, combining into packs to gallop and play, splitting up to return to their respective mothers at feeding time.

Commercial pig food is no good for wild pigs. They get an organic diet of oats, wheat, barley, soya meal and 'masses of vegetables'. The finished pigs are taken directly to Mr Joe Simpson's slaughter house and killed at once. The meat goes to hotels and restaurants. Demand has so far exceeded supply. A farm shop is being opened for direct sales to the public. I have ordered half a pig.

Chris gets most of his sows from Germany and Denmark. The Danes run a great breeding scheme for wild boar, many of which are released to maintain the wild stock. The Danes love hunting, and prefer eating wild pigs. Most of their battery pig production comes to Britain. Hercules is a Danish boar: a fine young fellow of a mere 200 lbs. In the next sty is Brutus from Poland. Brutus weighs in at over 500 lbs. He is the size of a small pony, and has tusks longer than most forefingers. Polish boars are the biggest, wildest and fiercest. In the shed a young sow had produced her first litter: one piglet. Mother and son were having tremendous games round the pen. It is not uncommon for the first litter to be eaten by the mother.

In the next pen some weaners were making strenuous efforts to catch the swishing tail of the cat which was sitting on the wall of the pen, contemptuously washing its paws: 'Pigs'll eat anything,' said Chris cheerfully. He told the tale of the York-shire lady who had gone in to feed her pen of Large Whites and must have slipped. Only her gumboots were found . . . .

Chris handles all the pigs from the beginning, which makes them very docile. We went to visit the pregnant ladies outside. Some new potatoes brought Fleur and Golden from their hut, their long snouts whiffling and eyes gleaming. In the next pen, Snork was happy to come out and have her tummy scratched. She rolled over and lay across Chris's feet in grunting ecstasy. It is a great thing to see a man doing a job he loves, and so obviously in tune with the animals he works with. The wild boar is a fascinating, attractive and highly intelligent animal. We both agreed that it would be wonderful to see them running wild in Britain again, perhaps in some of the larger forests, like Kielder. In the meantime Wilbore Farm is the place to see wild boar (domesticated).

# Chapter Forty-one

# BOARD STIFF

'Go,' THEY SAID, 'and learn to Windsurf.' I could hear
Them sniggering over the telephone. Some of you may
be Windsurfers (or Board Sailers). Almost all of you will have
seen the brightly coloured little sails and the lissom young
men and women skimming effortlessly across the sun-sparkling
sea. 'That looks rather fun' you probably said to yourself,
before slumping back into your deck-chair and taking another
slurp at your ice-cream cornet. It is rather fun.

Peter Clark runs Bearsports Outdoor Pursuits Centre in
Belford, Northumberland. He is a graduate in Physical Education and Outdoor Pursuits. He will take you canoeing, sailing,
rock-climbing, mountain biking: if it makes you wheeze and
wish that you were dead, then he will organize it for you. He
will also teach you to windsurf. He is going to windsurf across
the Irish Sea, later this year, in aid of the Marine Conservation
Society.*

Bearsports keep their aquatic gear in a functional wooden
hut, hard by the car-park at Beadnell, on the coast of Northumberland. The basic sailboard looks a bit like an ironing board.
It is made of moulded polyethylene. It is 3.75 metres long, and
about 80 cms at the widest, flat on top and modestly convex
at the bottom. There is a small stabilizing keel aft, and a
centre-board that can be raised or lowered amidships. Not that
windsurfers go in for blue-nosed nautical speak: they talk
about the front, back, and middle. It is on the middle of this
sliver of petrochemical by-product that you have to learn to

---

* At the time of writing Peter has not yet made it across the Irish Sea,
due to circumstances beyond his control.

balance. Some people are graced with natural balance. Some people are naturally graceless. I come in category two.

Then, of course, there is a sail. It is a simple triangular sail through one side of which the mast is thrust like a tent pole. The sail is tensioned out in the middle of a hoopla-shaped boom, which is what the punter hangs on to, trims his sail with, and steers by, as he skims across the briny. The mast is plugged into the board with a sort of universal joint, which means that the mast can be moved every which way and falls flat in the water with the sail if you let it go. Under extreme provocation the mast foot may jump out of its socket and catch you neatly in the criggs. This, as Peter cheerfully points out, is cheaper for Bearsports than breaking the mast.

The beaches of the Northumbrian coastline are magnificent sweeps of relatively empty sand. The reason that they are empty is the North Sea. The North Sea is high-case COLD. Those who go down to the sea on sailboards wear wetsuits. A wetsuit is a figure-hugging coverall made of insulating neoprene, and it makes no concessions to the figure. A fat man who has struggled into a thin man's wetsuit can have no illusions left.

The best way to learn is to get on and do it. Practice makes perfect, they say. It is like learning to ride a bicycle, they say. So down to the sea we trudged with boards and sails and several fathoms of rope with a concrete block on the end. This is attached to the beginner's board, and prevents him becoming a hazard to shipping somewhere off the Dogger Bank.

'Just carry on and practise in your own time,' says Peter. 'Take it easy.' He pushes his own board out, hops on, pulls up the mast and sail and is immediately sailing with graceful ease; it looks so easy.

Right then: hands flat on the centre line of the bobbing board and either side of the foot of the mast and sail, which lie flat on the water to leeward. An easy spring brings the knees aboard and on to the centre-line. Grasp the rope that will pull the mast up. Leap lightly to the feet, with the instep across the centre-line. Haul up the mast and sail. Grasp the mast so that the mast and the body form a graceful V. Tilt the mast until the bow swings to whatever destination you might be aiming for; like Sweden. Grasp the boom. The wind fills the sail and hey presto, you are sailing! Such is the theory.

I got my knees on, and fell off, again and again and. . . . Eventually I managed to struggle to my feet and stood wobbling clutching the rope.

'God loves a trier,' said the watchful Peter as he swept by.

I lost count of how many times the cold grey sea closed over my head, but at last I managed to get the mast up and stood there wobbling and juddering. 'The sploshes seem to be less frequent,' said Peter. He spoke too soon.

The mast was up. The board was level. Very gingerly I put hand to the boom and pulled in. The wind filled the sail and suddenly we were moving. I was sailing. I Was Sailing! I Was . . . Oh ££&*!! SPLOSH!

'An Excess of Icy Immersions equals Hexhaustion and Hypothermia.' Then the best thing to do is to go back to the hut and have a brew of tea. Then you can try again.

I should like to try again. Windsurfing is exciting and comparatively cheap. It is often possible to hire equipment by the day. You can purchase a basic board and a wetsuit for something like £400. All you then need is a roof-rack on your car and the oceans of the world are yours for the sailing. Most young people could acquire the basics of sailing a board in one day. For those, like me, who are victims of 'age, vice and unsoundness' it might take a little longer. It is undoubtedly worth taking a training course, if only to learn that the sea is not user-friendly and is certainly not a place for the ignorant or the foolhardy. In windsurfing, as in life, happiness is often a matter of using your head and keeping your balance.

# Chapter Forty-two

# FISH FARMERS HAVE BIG MUSSELS

Fish farming in Scotland was originally intended to offer the crofting community a chance to farm the sea. The pollution-free waters off the west coast of Scotland seemed ideal. The Highlands and Islands Enterprise Board offered generous grants for the establishment of fish farms, and the Crown Estates (who own the sea bed) ladled out leases with an open hand. There was no stampede of crofters to take up this new idea. They tended to pour another dram, put a few more peats on the fire and think about it. Haste is a rare commodity in the west of Scotland. Others were quicker to rush in.

English people who have emigrated to Scotland in search of the simple life are referred to as 'White Settlers': it is not a term of endearment. Many settlers thought that fish farming might be simple, and many of them have failed. The Multi National predators scented the blood in the water and came swooping in. They gobbled up the small fry, and also scooped up great shoals of Crown leases on their own account. They are now the major players in fish farming.

Fish farming has to be divided into 'fin' and 'shell': the greatest of these by far is 'fin', and at the moment this means Salmon. Salmon farming looks deceptively easy. The salmon are reared in great netting tanks suspended in sheltered sea lochs. They swim about getting plump on a regular intake of high protein pellets. Last year the industry produced some 50,000 tons of farmed salmon, and lots of troubles.

The first of the troubles is the current ex-farm price for salmon, which is profitless at around £1.30 per lb. Then there is predation by seals and poaching. On isolated farms whole tanks of fish have been siphoned off by sneaky trawlers. In some cases whole floating farms have been towed away.

The greatest problem of all is disease. Farmed salmon are very susceptible to stress. Stress produces jolly-sounding things such as Furunculosis, Infective Pancreatic Necrosis and Enteric Red Mouth Disease, to name a few. All this means that the fish have to be regularly treated with antibiotics. These are administered either in the food or by dunking the fish in treatment tanks. It stands to reason that what goes into a fish one way is going to come out in another. The question is: what is this doing to the marine environment? As yet, no one has come up with any firm answers.

John Anglesea is one of the few independent salmon farmers. He farms on the beautiful Loch Etive. He has degrees in Zoology and Fish Nutrition. John likes fish, but has approached the matter in a business-like and scientific way. He designed his own hatchery system, and breeds all his own parr (baby salmon), which helps him to control the problem of disease. The tiny parr are hatched in February, and reach a selling weight of about two kilograms in two years, with a survival rate of one in four. At the moment the farm sells 20,000 salmon a year, and employs four full-time people. John's business expertise and knowledge of pisciculture enables him to make a profit.

The saying goes that 'fin-fish farmers are usually failed academics; shellfish farmers are failed hippies'. There is not much of the hippy about Michael Picken. He is a retired marine biologist. In 1987 he and his partner, Peter Wormell, bought twelve acres of foreshore on Loch Creran, and took over a Crown Lease after the collapse of a previous oyster fishery.

There are currently about fifty oyster farms in Scotland, all run by owner/occupiers. At first sight, oyster farming looks pretty carefree. The oysters live in plastic net-bags laid out on metal grids between the high- and low-water mark. Oysters require neither feeding nor medication. They just lie there filtering the plankton from the sea and growing to their eighty-gram selling weight. They are then worth eighteen to twenty-five pence a piece, wholesale. The only exciting thing about an oyster (apart from eating it) is its sex life. They are hermaphrodite, being female one year and male the next. Oysters need Grade One clean water. Early farms were devastated by the effects of Tributoltin anti-fouling paint on boats and salmon cages. The biggest horror of oyster farmers now is the toxic algae (*Alexandrium tamarensis*). The oysters can absorb the toxin and take no hurt. Those who eat a toxic oyster will regret it before they die. The toxic algae is a recent phenomenon surrounded by mystery, suspicion and rumour. Oyster farm work has to go with the tides. The small oysters are kept at 10,000 to a bag, the larger at 1,000. The oysters need continuous grading and sorting. Oyster farmers do it in waders.

For ten years Walter Speirs worked in the catering business. Now his kitchen pallor has gone. Lean, brown and invincibly cheerful, he works long days at his mussel farm on Loch Etive. Mussels are helpful little creatures. Rafts are set out in the loch with thirty-feet ropes trailing down into the water. The 'spats' (minuscule baby mussels) cling naturally to the ropes and grow; there are eighty ropes on each raft. One raft will produce five tons of mussels per annum. Two gallons of mussels are worth £4.50 ex-farm. Money for reasonably new rope, you might think? Walter used to work a fourteen-hour day, six days a week. Each rope had to be hauled by hand. The mussels were then graded and washed manually. Now he has built a raft with outboard engine, a splendid Heath Robinson-esque crane to lift the ropes, and a Spanish machine washes and grades the mussels.

There can be a living, and there is plenty of hard work in fish farming, but as one man said: 'You have to remember that your work is always in the hands of God and nature and that manual labour is not a Spanish waiter.'

Chapter Forty-three

# A TOPPING END TO A LOAD OF RUBBISH

THE POSTMAN THOUGHT it highly amusing. The letter was addressed to 'The Person Responsible For International Shipping' at my address in Northumberlg (*sic*). This would seem to add a whole new dimension to my little farm. It makes me think that I ought to be investigating purchase of a small container vessel, if I am to continue to hold my head high. The trouble is that the size of vessel that would fit in the Powburn is not going to make much of an inroad into the Pacific Basin trade, which is one of the options mentioned. Anyway, I do not think that it is worth a big worry. The worry must be about the commercial sense of a company who would bother to send me half a forest's worth of glossy paper on the subject of International Shipping. I fear that it has wasted time and paper. Sheep will continue to go in the trailer; my scribblings will go through the fax machine, and the glossy brochure will go in the bin. Hang about though: I will send it to Fred, who tried to cross a flooded ford last Old Year's Night. His car went down-river towards the sea. He might like to hear about the Pacific Basin.

It is a Topping time down on the farm. By the beginning of August my pastures are rank with thistles (only good land grows thistles), nettles and tufts of coarse grass. Sheep like short, palatable grass. So now is the time when I give the pastures a shave, which should ensure a nice smooth sward for the autumn grazing. I do this with 'Henry the Honda', my ATV. An All Terrain Vehicle is a four-wheeled motorbicycle. Henry is bright red, has a 300cc engine and permanent four-wheel drive on his enormous low-ground pressure tyres. He thus has no trouble pulling a flail-mower with its own eleven-horsepower engine. The engine is also by Honda, and please take the matter up with the British Engineering Industry and not with me.

With the mower chattering and flailing away, we chug up and down, masticating thistles, pulverizing nettles and leaving sweet short grass where before was old and sour. The 'we' includes my Australian sheep dog, Oz, whose delight it is to ride on Henry's rear platform, looking smug. I have to admit that I find this a most satisfying and therapeutic job after a morning processing words. The sun and the breeze soothe the fevered brow. With the pipe drawing nicely one can ponder profound matters such as the meaning of life and what might be for dinner. There are birds and butterflies to observe. I can see how Pat is getting on with his hay on one side, and see the back end of Roland sticking out of the entrails of his combine on the other.

Who says that country life is boring? The country buzzes with activity and we are where it's at, Henry, Oz and I.

Knackers are starting to impinge upon the public consciousness. A 'knacker' is the carcase of a farm animal that has handed in its feed bucket for the last time. Those who keep livestock accept the fact that a certain number are going to decease during the year. There is then a disposal problem. This problem used not to exist. The farmer (when he had finished scratching his head and prophesying ruin) rang up the local hunt. Later that day a van would drive up. Old Buttercup would be winched on to the back and driven away.

Back at the Kennels the flesh would become *plat du jour* for the hounds. The hides, bones and offal would be sold on to become leather, bonemeal, grease and such like. BSE and the threat of new EC regulations have put a stop to this useful arrangement. Instead of being paid for the waste, hunts are now being charged up to £100 per ton to get it taken away. To put this in perspective, some of the bigger hunts in stock-rearing areas can easily have fifty-plus tons to dispose of every week. They cannot bear this financial burden. Some hunts have started charging farmers for a service that used to be free. Some have given up collecting carcases altogether. This leaves the carcase and the problem with the farmer.

MAFF wrinkled its fastidious nose and said it was none of its business; the responsibility for disposal of 'fallen livestock' lay with the farmer. The Ministry gives the farmer an official choice of burning or burying. Few, if any, farmers have incineration facilities, and if public incinerators exist, then I for one have never heard of them. Bury it then, says the Ministry. Have you (has that Nice Mr Gummer) ever tried digging a hole big enough to bury a sheep properly (let alone a cow), and have the environmental consequences of burial been thought through? The number of carcases to be disposed of annually probably runs into seven figures.

It is regrettable that some farmers have tried to solve the problem by going out at night and dumping it in someone else's ditch or wood. However, dumping the problem is exactly what the MAFF has been doing heretofore. It is time for a proper solution to this rotten problem, otherwise the whole stinking mess is likely to land in Mr Gummer's lap. That should concentrate his mind wonderfully.*

* At the time of going to press the situation has settled down, and the price of offal has increased somewhat. New methods of incineration have eased the disposal problems.

Chapter Forty-four

# CAN QUANGOROOS SING?

SOMETIMES IF THE night is still, I can lie in my bed and listen to hounds singing in their kennel a mile-and-a-half away. To me this is a magical sound, and must put £10,000 on the value of any property within earshot. It has to be said that not everyone feels the same. A lady who was new to the country complained about 'the dogs howling at night'. I gently pointed out that hounds had been there for generations and had every right to sing. The Environmental Health Officer told her much the same, but well wrapped up in 'officialese'.

The thing is that hounds only sing when they are happy. The nocturnal chorus is a sign of high morale, and if it does not happen, then there is something wrong. They do not sing every night, however. It can happen at any time, but as the autumn and hunting get nearer, the singing increases. The night before the start of hunting, which hounds always sense, they will be at it all night.

It is always started by a single hound, then more and more tune in until the kennel has its collective muzzle raised to the heavens. The sound soars to a crescendo, then gradually subsides. There will be silence, then another hound will strike up and the music will swell again. Music it is, because hounds always sing in harmony. The singing is always tuned to the note of the hound who starts. In the days when I lived at the Kennels I could get full benefit of this wonderful, wild, eerie sound. Those days are gone from me, but, Bless their Hearts, I still love to hear them sing.

The docking of dogs' tails may be banned.* I am all for

* As of July 1993 it will be illegal for anyone − including breeders − except a qualified vetinerary surgeon to dock dogs' tails.

banning such a practice. A dog's tail is as vital a bit of social gear as the mouth is in the human. The canine tail registers joy and misery, anger and submission. The dog smiles and scowls with its tail. My Rottweiler has to make do with a pathetic stump, and it is sad to see the poor chap desperately trying to waggle it. The tail has other important functions. Watch my collies playing and it is obvious how important the tail is in balancing, steering and braking at speed.

Some apologists for docking say that working dogs, such as spaniels, would damage their tails in thick covert if they were not docked. This is nonsense. The foxhound spends more time in thorns and brambles than most canines, without taking any hurt. You do quite often see hounds with very little hair on the tips of their sterns (hounds have sterns, dogs have tails). They wear the hair off by lashing the stern against their flanks when revelling in the scent of the fox. The tips can become sore, but this is easily treated, and is certainly no reason for docking.

Docking is a fashion-inspired mutilation. It is done to please the vanity of the show-bench brethren, and it is high time that it stopped. Then this sorry tale will have a happy ending for all dogs.

One of the most successful new creatures in our countryside is the Quangoroo. The Quangoroo is divided into two sub-species: the 'Alists and the 'Ologists. It is inevitable that the quango which spawned them will have either 'Nature' or 'Country' (preferably both) somewhere in its title. These gentle, rumpled creatures all tend to be bearded, earnest, well-meaning tunnel-visionaries. Brightly kagooled, they stumble about the country, falling over their clip-boards and causing a great deal of well-intentioned devastation. For instance, there was the occasion when the 'Alists lowered so many 'Ologists down the cliff face to inspect the Rare Raptor's nest that the mother took the huff and deserted it. Of course no one meant this to happen and it was all done to further the cause of conservation of wildlife, which is undoubtedly a righteous cause.

The countryside is not the natural habitat of the Quangoroos. They are far more at home in the sort of committees, symposia and conferences where the 'Chair' is not something that is sat on. A friend of mine has to attend a lot of these happenings for his work and his sins. He says that one of the fascinating things about Quangoroos is their quaint patois. He supplied me with a typical example: 'The defecatory habits of the sheep inhibit the integrity of the acaridau heath habitat.' This may be construed as 'Sheep doings kill moss'.

I climbed the Cheviot (2,500 feet and steep with it) the other day. It was two years since my last ascent, and it was obvious that an increasing number of people had done the same climb. Two brightly coloured parties of walkers overtook me. I admired their ambulatory zeal from the comfortable bank of heather where I was having a quiet look at the day. I especially admired the elderly man who was able to walk up Cheviot and dispense a non-stop stream of 'countryside lore' to his companions at the same time: his knowledge may have been suspect, but his keenness was not in doubt. This very keenness is beginning to present problems, however.

There was always a well-defined path up the hill, but now it is ten, fifteen, twenty feet wide in places, and erosion is in progress. Does it matter? After all it is only rough hill ground. Look at it another way: pause for a moment on your upward path and get out your Boys' Own Combined Compass and Calculator. Five miles of six-feet-wide beaten track equals just over $3\frac{1}{2}$ acres. That means the destruction of 150 acres of grazing for which men are paying a rent. Surely they should be compensated? But by whom? Aye, masters, there's the rub.

Chapter Forty-five

# A RARE SIGHT INDEED

WHAT DO ALDERNEY Cattle, Mayo Mountain Sheep and Dorset Gold-Tip Pigs have in common? The answer is that they are all extinct.

Over the centuries a great number of different breeds of cattle, sheep, pigs and poultry evolved in the British Isles. These were mostly fairly local, and were produced to cope with local conditions and local needs. At least twenty breeds have disappeared since 1900. Some were shouldered aside by, or absorbed into, breeds deemed more suitable for modern farming methods and consumer demand. Some just went out of fashion. Farmers can be as fashion-conscious as any teenager when it comes to off with the old and on with the new. However, some farmers clung stubbornly to their old favourites; some prominent agriculturists reasoned that these old breeds were not just oddities, but precious gene banks whose qualities might once again be needed (and anyway they rather liked the look of the funny old things). In 1973, the Rare Breeds Survival Trust was set up and based at the National Agricultural Centre at Stoneleigh, Warwickshire. It is alive and well.

Every year, in the first week of September, the RBST holds its Show and Sale at Stoneleigh. It is a fascinating occasion, not least because the Rare Breeders are worthy of study themselves. You are likely to encounter every type from Emaciated Flower Child to Weather-beaten Baronet. They are all dedicated to their animals.

Mrs Annabel Holt is devoted to her Irish Moiled (polled) Cattle. This attractive red and white breed is down to 150 breeding females, although a hardy and reliable dairy and suckler cow. It just went out of fashion. The RBST have it on the Category One (Critical) list. Mrs Holt also has Leicester Longwool sheep, which are Category Two (Endangered). The rest of her time is spent saving whales and rain forests: right on to that, Sister! Thank goodness someone has got the time and the oomph to do it. However, it was obviously a mistake to suggest that her Leicesters would produce a good heavy-weight butcher's lamb.

Time to investigate the trade stands and experience true eclecticism: moccasins, pork/herb/garlic sausages, home-made jewellery, *The Complete Works of William Shakespeare, Hunting: an Introductory Guide*, sweat-shirts with sheep jokes, spinning wheels, lamb sausages with coriander and rugs'n'quilts. There is also everything a shepherd might want, from foot-rot shears to elastrators (you do not want to know). A lady stall-holder found time to commune with a quiet pot of yoghurt, whilst another fought the flies off her home-made fudge with bared teeth and an enormous carving knife.

A wander and a wonder through the sheep lines and unfamil-iar sights and names: Boreray (tiny 'primitive' horned sheep), North Ronaldsay (tiny primitives again, whose basic diet is seaweed) and the magnificently horned Portlands. The Cots-wold is a breed that dates back to Roman times. Its wool helped to build the fortunes of mediaeval England. Then came a stab of nostalgia for the scenes of my youth — the Greyface Dartmoor (Category Four: At Risk) — splendid stocky, woolly little sheep, bred for the rigours of the Moor.

And there was John Mead, a friend of thirty years whom I had not seen for twenty-five. John had brought 115 sheep to the show. He still maintains his 150-ewe flock on the edge of Dartmoor. His grandfather started the flock and his daughter, Jennifer (Secretary of the Breed Association), is the fourth generation of Greyface Flockmasters.

'Why, I minds you when you was just a little maid,' said I, dropping back into the vernacular.

'I minds you too, Bill Poole; you used to shout a lot.'

'Yere, Bill, do 'ee mind the time that us . . .,' and John and I were off again with the Dartmoor Hounds: *eheu fugaces!*

The Longhorn cattle were in the show ring. I love these

massive, gentle animals with their brindle colouring and sweeping horns. I have a secret desire to have a small herd one day. They may be slow to mature, but they will produce superb beef on nothing much but good grass. The Lady Judge was also greatly to be admired: a superb example of British Agricultural Womanhood.

The party of schoolchildren next to me joined in the bellowing with the bulls.

'Uuugh! he's slobbering!'

'He's got rabies! Miss! Miss! He's got rabies!'

'No, he hasn't,' said the long-suffering teacher. 'You need a ring through your nose, Danny Smith!'

Daisy Rudrick and Roy Barling were there with their White-faced Woodland sheep. They farm forty acres near Brackley. 'We're SOILERS,' said Roy, beaming through his beard and waving a chicken leg (give up? It stands for 'Sold Out In London, Enjoying Rural Splendour'). He was in Electronics. She was in Information Management. They keep seven breeds of rare sheep, as well as cows, ducks, cats and chickens, but the farming slump may drive them back to town: 'It's that Seldom Glummer,' said Roy.

The Greyface Dartmoor ewes were in the ring with a most athletic judge. In spite of his natty suiting and bowler hat, he would sometimes drop to all fours and minutely inspect the undercarriages. John Mead very properly won first prize. It has to be said that the dedication and enthusiasm of the Rare Breeders is not always matched by skills in stockmanship. This showed with some of the exhibits.

Mrs Holt got Reserve Champion with her Leicester Longwool Ram Lamb. As we said goodbye, she promised me some literature on Saving the World: 'I'm not mad, you know, I just think differently.' This might almost be a motto for the Rare Breeds Survival Trust; thank God, say I, for people who think differently: we might save the world yet.

# Chapter Forty-six

# OF LAMBS AND HOUNDS AND NAPPIES

THIS IS THE time of year when lambs are going to the slaughter. 'Ugh!' say People. 'Don't talk about it: I don't want to think about it.' They — we — ought to think about it, especially if holding a delicately poised forkful of meat at the time. That piece of meat once had four legs and feelings. The transition should concern us all.

I used to take pride in my lambs. From the moment of conception through to the moment they left the farm, it was my small conceit that my lambs had the best care and attention that my skills and experience could give them. It was good to see bright-eyed, good-skinned, full-bellied lambs stotting and playing up and down the hedge backs. There was great satisfaction to me as a stockman in their well-being and contentment. Were they otherwise it would not only be an offence to my pride but also bad business: a happy animal is a potentially profitable animal.

So far, so good, but now comes the tricky part. Did I have qualms about sending my lambs to be killed? I have no qualms about the purposeful and useful killing of animals, always provided that the act is quick, clean and involves minimal stress. The ideal would be to slaughter the lambs on the farm. As things stand, this option is hardly possible.

At one time I could load butcher-fit lambs on to my trailer at 0830 and trail them fifteen miles down the road to the local slaughter house. They would be killed by midday. Things are different now. New EC regulations regarding slaughter houses are so bureaucratically irksome, and the costs of implementing them so savage, that many smaller plants are closing down. Eventually there will only be a handful of large abattoirs to serve the whole country. This means that it might be forty-eight hours (even more, if the lambs go for export) from the farm-gate to the killing plate. This must involve stress and suffering. Apart from the animal welfare aspect, this is bad for you, the consumer; stress affects the quality of the meat.

'Ahha!' say the Meat Men. 'It is all a question of Economics of Scale. Joe Public wants cheap meat.' Perhaps Joe does, but is he getting it? At the time of writing, ex-farm lamb prices continue to slide. A prime butcher's lamb is worth between £25 and £30 at the farm-gate (including subsidy); not much for a year's work. Now I hear of retail prices of around £2.45 per lb. This would put the lamb in at about £110. Who is getting value for money?

Hunting is well underway in the north. In the early stages, hounds tend to go right out into the deep hills far away from the harvest. This is a country of straggling conifer blocks, glutinous peat haggs and huge, boulder-strewn bracken beds. The going varies from 'rough, a bit' to 'bad, a bit'. I am full of admiration for the way the hill shepherds negotiate this jumbled terrain on their farm bikes. Bitter experience has taught me to leave this to the experts. It is boots and stick for me, with a mouthful of tea and an egg sandwich in my shoulder bag.

Mind you, even in this wilderness the sportsman will not be entirely without other refreshment. I was standing in the yard of a lonely steading at 0630 one morning, watching hounds hunting slowly along the opposite hill. The door opened and a man in a pair of Y-fronts appeared. He was rubbing his eyes with one hand. The other hand held what subsequently turned out to be a half-pint tumbler of nearly neat whisky. Without a word he thrust the glass into my hand and disappeared back into the house. Hospitality is taken seriously in the hills.

The weather should always be taken seriously in the hills. The other morning I had climbed out to about 1,500 feet when the fog came down with awful suddenness. The world disappeared. I was on a rough track of sorts so I kept on. I could hear hounds occasionally far away on my right. Then they too disappeared and the world was a swirling silence. I sweated doggedly on, up and up. Then a dark shape loomed out of the fog. It was a man coming the other way.

'Have ye hord the hoonds?' we both said simultaneously.

'Na,' we both said simultaneously. Then as suddenly as it had come, the mist rolled back. There were the hounds, far away on the side of a huge heather basin, still hunting steadily. Beyond them the great purple, brown and green hills rolled away, bright and crisp and clear. We leant on our sticks. 'Man,' said my friend, 'was there ever a bonnier sight than yon?' There was no arguing with that. 'Mind,' he said, 'it's arl the bonnier for the hoonds being in it.' I could not argue with that either.


A friend of mine is a professional dog handler who specializes in 'difficult' dogs. A very smart lady came to see him the other day tugging along a reluctant package of canine neuroses. The patient was a Bleu de Gascogne, a beautiful blue-mottled breed of French hound. This unfortunate bitch had been kept in a flat half-way up a tower block and made to wear 'Pampers'; small wonder it was bonkers. After a rehabilitation period, my friend sent the bitch to a pack of foxhounds. She is now calm and happy and doing what comes naturally.

# Chapter Forty-seven

# LIFE ON THE FRONTIER

NORTHUMBERLAND IS THE nicest part of England to live in. One of the reasons for this is that it is very difficult to get to live there unless you live there already. In case this statement makes you scratch your head a bit, I will try to explain. Northumberland is still pleasantly feudal. The local families have been very successful at hanging on to their property and remaining in houses that may evoke thoughts of Euston Station. The houses tend to be surrounded by broad acres with commodious farm steadings. These are inhabited by tenant farmers and shepherds, whose forebears rode with the forebears of the Squire in the ancient Border sports of murder, rapine and cattle-lifting. These old Border urges have now been sublimated into foxhunting and Rugby Football.

All of this means that it is not easy for an offcomer to gain a property toe-hold in this desirable area. The Des Gent's Res with 4/5 bed, 2 rec, study, hall, usual offices, stables and a small block of land is almost non-existent. The Dower Houses contain Dowagers. Younger sons are encouraged to come home for the family shoot, but not to set up house.

I am an offcomer. I moved to Northumberland in 1982 and it took me five years to find some property of my own. The first base was a stable cottage, loaned by a benevolent land-owner. From there my wife and I ranged far and wide. We wanted a farm. I wanted a hill farm. The wife wanted a not-so-hill farm. We would rent or buy. The estates tend to have the admirable policy of favouring established estate families for their tenants. Farms are sometimes let outwith the family system, and on these occasions the rents tend to be alarming. What would you consider to be a sensible rent for a hard, high, heather farm? Might you go as high as £5 per ewe? My information is that such a farm has just been let for £11 per ewe. Even higher rents for hill farms have been bruited about. The National Park/Social Payment factor is part of the sum, but even so you may wish to shake your head and wonder.

We did our own share of head shaking. I think we looked at ten farms, good, bad and indifferent. With each farm we did a very careful costing on what it was worth, with due consideration to its commercial potential. We also took the potential cost of sorting the house out – one person's habitude can mean another's complete refurbishment. In every case our offers were considered risible. To give one example: a freehold farm that I had valued at £170,000 subsequently went for over £250,000. The others went for apparently inflated prices.

The purchasers came in two categories. The farm quoted above was bought by an established local owner/occupier with two sons. I imagine that he could average the price out over his two properties and justify it thus.

Then there was the 'Hampshire' factor. 'Hampshire' is the local term for those who have sold business, or broad acres, in the south and come north to seek *lebensraum* with a crisp wad of roll-over in the back pocket. Even inflated Northumbrian prices looked like monopoly money to these people, and good luck to them. We suffered much disappointment at the time, but with hindsight, the Hampshires did me a good turn. Farming was feeding high on the pig's back then, and the banks were stuffing fistfuls of the folding stuff down the agricultural shirt-front. Times have changed. Had we bought any of those farms, the family Poole would now be in trouble.

We rented a redundant farm-house. This was not easy, but it was possible. At that time some landowners were keen on taking land in hand when tenancies became vacant. That fine flush of enthusiasm seems to be wearing off.

Many Northumbrian farm-houses are splendid dwellings. Many were rebuilt or added to in Victorian times, to the greater glory of the estate and its incumbent. Fine houses indeed, if you can afford to heat them. The Northumbrian climate is hard, clean and bracing: a good deep breath reams out the lungs: that is summer. In winter the south-east wind revs up in the mountains of Russia, gains venom and bone-chilling nastiness over the North Sea, and meets Northumberland head on. Those lovely, decorative Victorian sash windows are no match for it.

I rented ground for my sheep, wherever I could find it. There was one small block of land which enchanted me. It ran down to a little burn. On the other side the ground swept up to the Cheviots. I used to lean on my stick, below the little wood, and stare at this view and think what a wonderful place it would be to build a house, if only I could buy that bit of land.

Two years later I did just that, and built a house where my stick had rested. It is not a typical Northumbrian house. It is small and snug. It is double-glazed, centrally heated, draught-free, and it is all on one level. 'Ahha!' people say. 'You built a bungalow.' It would be quite unthinkable for a Northumbrian Master of Foxhounds to live in a Bungalow, so it is a 'Single-Storey Dwelling', and it has the finest view in England.

Chapter Forty-eight

# LET'S STALK A RAMBLER IN GREEN WELLIES

I WAS INTERESTED to read about the recent mass trespass by the Ramblers' Association, and I thought to myself, 'What is right for the Ramblers must be right for the Rambled (on)'. So when I have nothing better to do (it could be quite some time), it is my intention to assemble a merry band of stalwart fellow Peasants. We shall put on our flat caps and tackety boots. We shall assemble crates of ale and bales of sandwiches. We shall hire a char-à-banc. Then with many an earthy quip and rustic song we shall drive to wherever the Ramblers' Association hangs its collective rucksack. There we shall ramble all through the offices of the organization. What fun we shall have. We shall scatter our sandwich papers and beer cans. We shall leave doors open so that all the typists escape and mill about bleating and blocking the traffic. I shall whip out the megaphone that I just happen to have in my bait bag and make an impassioned speech about the burgeoning perils of 'Green Fascism'. The lads will all cheer lustily and we shall sing *The Happy Wanderer* (unauthorized version) all the way home. It all sounds rather fun, this trespass lark. Anyone like to knit me a bobble hat?

At the beginning of October I usually try to have a week of hill-stalking. The red deer are one of the great glories of the Scottish Highlands; they are also a major economic resource in an area which has more scenery than economy. The forest that I visited is a wild and magnificent wilderness of rock and heather and peat haggs – wonderful to look at and totally useless except for the harvest of red deer. This harvest provides employment for two stalkers and two pony men. Without it the glen would be uninhabited.

I like to claim that I am fairly fit, but the first two days' stalking are always an agony of aching legs and bursting lungs, whilst the stalker just strolls nonchalantly up the one-in-two slope, with his hands in his pockets. Oh, the blessed relief when he stops to 'spy' the opposite hill. Even with the naked eye it is possible to see that the hill is dotted with feeding deer. The telescope is closed with a snap. There are stags there 'right enough', but they are all young beasts. Their time is not yet.

The stalker's art is to find a suitable cull beast, then get the 'Rifle' (the punter) to within 150 yards without being seen, smelt, or heard. This can mean hours of hard walking, aching climbs and then the crawling: 'Upon thy belly shalt thou go'; in the burns, through slimy peat haggs, across trembling falls of scree. All of this may come to nothing. A curl in the wind, a careless movement, a clatter of a stone and the deer are away. But the time will come when the stalker slips the rifle from its cover, gingerly eases a round into the chamber, checks the safety catch and slides it across: 'Yon muckle beast ahint the twee hinds.'

To take the shot it is necessary to wait until the stag is standing broadside on and clear of other deer. It can be an exercise in patience. I once lay in the firing position for two hours. A properly placed shot means instantaneous death. A triumph of blood lust? Not from me; but certainly the satisfaction of a difficult job well done. That might help to sustain me on the weary walk down the glen with the merry Highland rain sluicing down the neck. As does the thought that the carcase strapped across the deer saddle on the pony is the finest organically produced meat that anyone can eat: a true Harvest of the Hills.

There are a great many glossy magazines with *'Country'* in their titles. Magazine Country has nothing to do with rural reality. It is a never-never land where the Archers live and polish their green wellies. The fantasy is also reflected in the adverts for Country Clothing and the people who model them. Take a gentleman from any typical magazine ad. He is modelling a smart country coat. He carries a gun rather preciously. His dog looks suspiciously stuffed. Everything is smooth and unsullied, from the young man's unlined face to his squeaky clean rubber boots (green, of course).

Perhaps advertisers should consider the Field Credibility of their glossy pictures. Suppose the chap had the sort of complexion that only years of wind, weather and whisky can produce. We might give him a moustache as well. Let us put a bit of wear on the coat, rip a sleeve and replace the belt with a bit of baler twine. We will give him the sort of tweed cap that looks like a trampled muffin. Now some cartridges in the pocket to make the coat baggy; that is better. The slim-line 'breeks' will have to go; we want some nice baggy plus-fours: sort of thing you can slip a ferret down. Now we will finish off with heavily tacketed ankle-boots and gaiters. Oh yes, and we will stick a pipe in his gob. Now that looks much more the thing. That will really sell the product and the funny thing is that the chap now looks remarkably like me: any offers?

Chapter Forty-nine

# JOHN PEEL LIVES, O.K.?

'ARE YE GANNIN' to the Opening Hunt?' asked the taxi driver. 'Lucky bugger; I wish I could gan.' With his earrings, beard and pigtail he did not fit the standard image of a foxhunter, but then who does? What did he think of those who wanted to stop hunting? 'They're nowt but rubbish. . . .'

I was on my way to the Opening Meet of the Blencathra Foxhounds at the Salutation Inn, Threlkeld, Cumbria. The Blencathra hunt the country that was hunted by John Peel. The Lake District with its fells and crags is too steep for horses. Like all the 'fell packs' the Blencathra are hunted and followed on foot. You may think that this indicates a certain hardiness on the part of the followers, and you would be right. There is a no-nonsense approach to foxhunting in these bleak hills. The packs are organized and maintained by farmers for the express purpose of killing the foxes who kill the hill lambs, the main source of the hill farmers' income. You do not believe that foxes kill lambs? I know that they do, but you should go and argue the point with the fell men themselves: they are robust in argument. The fell packs each kill about one hundred foxes a season, which is deemed sufficient to preserve a natural balance. But that is not the whole story; the fell men hunt because they love the sport on the wild hills. The hunt also provides a catalyst for the social life of dances and other functions in this remote area.

Threlkeld is a tiny village that 'nestles' like a cliché at the foot of mighty Blencathra Fell. At least 300 people filled the little street, and the bars of the Salutation and the Horse and Farrier. There is no harm in an 0930 dram for people who are going to spend a day on the fells; anyway, there is no bad time to drink whisky: very good for the cholesterol.

It was unfortunate that the meet clashed with a Draft Ewe

Sale, which kept many farmers away, but the local ranks were swelled by visitors from all over England. There were people from Yorkshire, Devon, the New Forest and from Somerset. Many visitors arrange their holidays to have a week in the Lake District, hunting five or six days in the week. It was good to meet old friends.

The Blencathra has only had six masters since 1839. The present incumbents, Major P. L. Davidson and Mr G. B. Graham, have been in office since 1973 and carry on the proud tradition. Major Davidson is in his ninetieth year, and was a much respected architect in Keswick. Mr Graham is another Keswick man. He is now also taking his *otium cum*, but before that was a celebrated Q.C. and a renowned hill-walker.

There was a stir of excitement in the crowd as the hounds arrived, walking down the hill from the kennels with Barry Todhunter, the so-aptly named huntsman, and John Bell, the whipper-in. Here is another proud tradition. A Huntsman of Foxhounds is a respected figure in the local community, and nowhere more so than in the Lake District, where the huntsman is a Great Man. His doings become enshrined in song and story: look what happened to old John Peel.

Barry is only the fourth man to hunt the Blencathra since 1894. He was bred and buttered at Caldbeck (John Peel's home), and his family still farm there. He left school at fifteen to whip-in to the Lunesdale, moving to the Blencathra as whipper-in (huntsman's assistant) in 1973, aged seventeen. In 1985 a rock fall crushed 'everything except my head'. Only his amazing mental and physical toughness enabled the surgeons to save his life and return him to full health and fitness.

Barry's predecessor was the famous Johnny Richardson, who hunted the hounds for nearly forty years, and was still in office when he died in his sleep. In the Hitler War, Johnny was captured by the Germans in Italy and 'just walked out'. He kept walking through the Apennines until he eventually walked into the Allied lines. They are rugged men, these fell huntsmen. They hunt four days a week in the worst of hill weather. It would be interesting to know how many miles they walk in a hunting season. They all walk very slowly; or so it seems until you try to keep up with them. Barry is very conscious of the famous tradition. Although he is only in his fourth season, he has the huntsman's boots well filled.

Time to move off, but only one hundred yards, for the traditional stop at the Horse and Farrier. Then another one hundred yards before stopping at the house of Mrs Joyce Airey, forty years on the Blencathra Committee. Then came the last traditional call of the Opening Meet, at the village school. A blast on the horn brought the children tumbling out to line the roadside fence and lean over to pat the hounds.

'Who wants to blow the horn?' asked Barry.

'Me!' 'Me!' 'Me!' There were some very creditable noises, each greeted with a cheer from the crowd.

The politenesses were over: it was time for business. We climbed a steep, narrow track beside a rushing beck, and eventually debouched on to the open fell. There was time to have a good look at the followers. Who follows the Blencathra? It is much the same *mélange* as with the rest of Foxhunting Britain: take a pinch of Aristocracy – a weather-beaten Peer of the Realm, leaning on his 'horn-heid' stick – sprinkle some Commerce and Professions – a barrister, a brace of doctors, an inspector of constabulary. Take a double handful of a mixture that might include anything from a painter of beautiful water-colours to a man who delivers animal feed-stuffs. Decorate with lady school-teachers, a company director, a hairdresser and wives and girl friends. Then plonk the whole mix on a solid base of farmers, shepherds and farm workers. It would have been hard to tell one from another. All wore sensible drab clothing for hard weather and hard walking. In Lakeland only the huntsman wears a red coat.

That red coat had already become a red dot on the steep, sweeping side of Blencathra. Hounds were spread out, light-coloured specks amongst the tumbled rocks and many-hued bracken. The followers divided into groups. The hardy few, whose legs and lungs could stand the pace, followed the huntsman. The less ambitious turned along the track that followed the bottom of the hill. 1,000 feet or more above were scattered figures who had climbed 'high out' earlier on, and who kept disappearing in the clouds.

How do people on foot keep up with hounds when they find a fox and start to run? They do not. It is worth remembering that a hill hound may cover as much as 200 miles in a day's hunting. The art of following hounds on foot is to know the country and know the likely run of the fox. The experienced followers know that a fox seldom runs dead straight. They get high out and keep to the tops. They walk with the grain of the country and not against it. Experience allows them to cut corners and to keep going when hounds have disappeared from sight and hearing. Experience will bring them to the spot where they (hopefully) will see hounds 'coming in' on a distant hillside. Experience will also bring them safely off the hill, when the mist clamps down.

The wind that day was strong and north of east, bringing in the 'blue haze', which is hated by foxhunters; hounds hunt by scent, and there is never a scent with a blue haze and east wind.

Hounds had turned into a steep rocky ghyll. The huntsman was a tiny figure perched on a high crag, his well-pitched voice encouraging his hounds to spread and find a fox. On a distant scree-face a hound spoke, then another; the cry swelled, echoing from the rocky cliffs. An argument raged behind me as to which hound it was which had 'yon right squeaky voice'. There was distant shouting from a cloud-shrouded figure: the fox had 'gone ower top – yon way'. A grizzled man with two formidable-looking terriers sitting next to me on the hillside said: 'Aye, but which way's yon way? Can't see which way t'bugger's facing.' Hounds answered the question by disappearing into the cloud above the opposite face. To move or not to move? It is sometimes best to light the pipe and wait. Ten minutes later the faint cry of hounds came from the clouds: they were 'coming in'. Barry's screech told us that he had seen the fox, and there he was, slipping easily down through the brackens. Hounds came chiming out of the mist on the line.

It was not to be a great hunting day. The prophets had been right about the scent. Hounds and huntsman had to struggle. They were not alone. I was faced with a steep 'clim oot' to keep in touch. It did nothing for my morale to be overtaken by two middle-aged ladies and a little old man of seventyish, all moving easily. It was some miles and much

time later that I came up with hounds. They had 'holed' the
fox in rock face, which was deemed impregnable. The huntsman blew for home.

It was 5.30 when I got back to the Salutation. The singing
had already started. Singing is an essential part of *Après Chasse*
in Lakeland. Most of the songs are peculiar to the fells. They
are historical and biographical. All the great fell huntsmen
have songs written about them (John Peel, for instance, and
the proper tune is quite different). Great hunts are balladed;
famous terriers are hymned; gamecocks, Herdwick tups (rams),
collie dogs and all the life of the hills are recorded in song.
New songs are composed all the time and old ones updated.
There are also stories and recitations.

So the evening went, with a pause only for the 'Taity Pot
Supper'. Taity Pot is an ancient Cumbrian dish. Take some
mutton (heather-fed Herdwick, for choice) and put it in a
roasting dish; add onions, carrots, or whatever; cover with
slices of black pudding and potatoes; put in the oven and roast
slowly for two hours. I can tell you it puts the hairs back on
your chest after a day on the hill.

The evening warmed up. The weather-beaten faces got a little
redder. Coats came off. The smoke got thicker. The room was
packed. A chairman was appointed to manage the festivities; a
man with a strong voice and a forceful personality. He banged
the floor with his stick: 'Right, lads! best of order! I say; BEST OF
ORDER!' The hubbub subsided. The format was immutable. A
singer was nominated; one singer, one song, was the rule,
although everyone joined in the choruses. The singer then 'called
on' his successor. The chairman ordered him to stand and deliver:

'C'mon, lad; ye're behind them pillars; can't see you, lad.'

'I'll mebbe's sing after a bit.'

'After a bit of what? Bugger that; stop ratching about, lad,
and get yerself out here.'

'. . . there was Dido, Bendigo, Gentry, they were there'o;
Traveller who never looked behind him; there was Countess,
Towler, Bonnylass and Prowler, these were the hounds that
would find him!!!' We all bellowed the final chorus and stamped
our boots and clapped in appreciation:

'I call on John X.'

'He's boogered now; he arnly knaws yan song and he's forgotten that.'

It mattered not how halting the delivery, or rasping the voice, every offering was listened to in reverential silence and received thunderous applause and stamping of tackety boots. So the evening went, and passed through night and into morning with good fellowship, banter and laughter.

Someone said: 'It's a pity yon bloody Kinnock isn't here; it might make him think different.'

'Nay,' said another, 'if he heard John, he'd likely want to ban singing as well as 'unting.'

Perhaps it would have done Mr Kinnock good to have been there that night, amongst those straightforward, hard-working folk. He might then have come to realize that foxhunting is part of the warp and woof of rural existence; that for all those people, the local hunt is not just a vital instrument of fox control, but a natural part of their everyday way of life. Yet it is that way of life that Labour seems determined to destroy. As another man said: 'They don't want to save the fox, they want to kill the countryman.' People like the men and women of Blencathra may not be as easily done away with as the politicians might wish.

# Chapter Fifty

# JUST RATCHING ABOUT IN FOUR-WHEEL DRIVE

I AM ALWAYS on the look-out for useful new words to add to my vocabulary. I discovered a good one in Cumberland: 'Ratch'. 'Ratch' means broadly the same as 'Scouse' in the West Country, or 'Rive' in the north-east; they can have subtly different meanings in different contexts. For instance: a stray dog can scouse (or rive) your in-calf heifers about the field; or you may be out all night riving (or scousing) about, and you really should know better at your age.

'Ratching about' can mean anything from walking down the lane with your hands in your pockets kicking stones, to scousing about doing all the things that you would not want your mother (or your wife) to hear about. So there you are. Next time we meet we will 'gan oot for a bit of a ratchet', and I hope that you will have your wallet with you; I always forget mine. It is an hereditary fault.

Hounds do not come across my farm very often. There has been little cover on the place to hold a fox heretofore. I have high hopes that when my new plantations grow and thicken, foxes will take up residence. I would dearly love to have a litter of cubs on the place. This is not just because I enjoy watching them, but because a resident vixen does offer a measure of protection. She would leave my game hens alone and would discourage interlopers from messing on her patch. Foxes always go away from home to kill. That is why my neighbour has been so smug about *his* vixen feeding her cubs on *my* hens.

I found the MFH rather smug about it too. I had him cornered at a Drinks Spotty, and complained about assassinations taking place under my bedroom window. 'Jolly good,' he said, 'keep up the good work,' and drifted away to talk to someone else. I really do not know what these young Masters are coming to; now in my day.... The violent demise of my best stud cock made me threaten to send a damage claim to the Hunt Poultry Fund, but as the Hunt Treasurer happens to be my wife, I knew that it would be like trying to squeeze moisture out of a breeze block.

The hounds were all round here last Saturday. There were foxes going all ways. The riders thundered across the farm and hounds killed a fox a field from the house.

I went up into the top field, which gives a good view-point, and watched from there with Moses. Moses is my sole remaining horse, and is now taking his honourable retirement. No horse loved hunting more than Moses. When he was out in front with the hounds, you could ride him with a thread, otherwise disc-brakes and an anchor would not hold him. He was a huntsman's horse. I thought he would be tearing about the field with excitement, but he was standing like a rock, his ears pricked, watching and listening. So we watched and listened together: just two old has-beens.

Sometimes when I am loitering along the streets of London, chewing one of the straws that I always keep behind my ear, I wonder at the number of 4 × 4 vehicles I see. I cannot help but wonder how many of these gleaming machines ever engage four-wheel drive, and whether those immaculate tyres (do they get polished?) remain innocent of good old English mud all their working lives.

Up here in the Borders, 4 × 4s are a fact of life. They are handy for nipping up muddy tracks to feed distant stock, for carrying the shoot luncheon, and even for popping down to the Four Jolly Knackermen to transact some vital bit of business. 4 × 4s are entirely necessary in the coming time of icy roads and likely snowfall. All wise persons carry a tow rope, a shovel and a survival blanket in their vehicle.

Even moderate snowfall cuts my house off, and the only way out is with four-wheel drive. Then I am on to roads which may have been ploughed-out, but which will then have become sheets of ice. Some people seem to believe that four-wheel drive will protect them against ice. The sad fact is that however many wheels are driving, if they have no traction then you are going to slide. There is little that you can do about it, except worry about the eight-wheeled quarry lorry that is coming sideways down the hill behind you.

Perhaps my thoughts about urban 4 × 4s have been unworthy. They probably come in very handy when the great blizzards sweep down from Swiss Cottage, and Sloane Street is hock-deep in mud. I think I might just go and ask that amazing lady who has uncoiled herself from a Range Rover whether she uses it to hay up her sheep on Hackney Marshes.

Talking of 4 × 4s, I am XL. To be absolutely truthful I am 3XL. In case you should want to revel in the statistics, I have a 50-inch chest, a 46-inch waist, and a 50-inch rear echelon; oh yes, and an $18\frac{1}{2}$-inch neck band. In short (well, six feet actually), I am a fine bit of Old English Beef who has extreme difficulty in finding clothes to fit me.

British manufacturers are convinced that 'the Man on the Clapham Omnibus' has a 38-inch chest and not much else. It is for him that they produce their clothing. On occasion they may just concede that there might be a few XL grotesques with 44-inch chests, but that is really their final offer. Do they not know that people have got larger? In the USA I can walk into any clothes shop and get what I want. Seventeen-stone weakling that I am, I am frequently dwarfed by some of the other customers. The Americans understand about the needs of the larger man, even unto and including his nether regions. American underpants are like the American character: generous and expansive: they truly provide peace of cod.

# Chapter Fifty-one

# 'NECK, KNEES AND NUTS'

'NECK, KNEES AND Nuts,' said Martin with terrifying cheerfulness, 'get 'em there and you can't go wrong. Now try the knife on him, Rod.' An ex-Royal Marine with a fighting knife concentrates the mind wonderfully; so: block, twist, lock, pressure on the wrist and backwards to the floor he has to go, the knife clattering away into a corner. Hang on to the wrist, foot in the armpit: 'That's it; now break his wrist and kick him; give him a bit of pain to think about. . . .'

All right, you can relax now. Rod and I are quite unblemished, save for some spectacular bruises in my case. It is all part of 'Situation Awareness and Self-Protection Training': who needs it? I do, you do, anyone who travels in these unsettled times does. Anyone could find themselves in a 'Conflict Situation'; it is not enough to rely on being lucky to get out of it.

Protection Training Assessment Ltd knows all about conflict situations. It is a specialist security company run by Bob, Martin, Rod and Lee, all ex-special forces. PTA operatives are all high-calibre persons. The firm recruits exclusively from such units as the Special Air Service, Special Boat Squadron and Royal Marines. They will teach you to *detect* potential trouble, to *deter* conflict by controlling the situation, but when push comes to shove, to *react* to physical attack and extract yourself.

The first day of my course was mostly theory. Most self-protection is common sense: it is better to keep out of trouble than get out of it. There are elementary precautions that all travellers may take. Check your hold baggage in late at airports, there is less time for baggage handlers to rifle it (endemic in certain countries). As there is no lock that cannot be picked, wedge the door of your hotel room. Buy a map of your destination and mark out your route in advance. Whenever possible find out the dangerous areas and mark them on your map also.

Agree the price for your taxi journey before you set off, and should the driver appear to be deviating from the planned route, then ask him why. Route planning also applies to hire cars (keep your doors locked and the windows up at all times), but if you do get yourself into a part of town where the vibes are bad, *do not* stop and ask the way, just keep driving until things look better. Do not hire a conspicuous car.

On foot, keep to well-lit streets and places where there are plenty of people. Avoid eye contact with strangers in the street, but if you do find some friendly natives who wish to liberate your watch, wallet and credit cards, your best choice is to hand them over. Always be alert and use your common sense; if a situation feels wrong, then it is wrong: get out. Suspicion may save your money and your life.

Each day of the course finished with a dose of 'Close-Combat'. Close-combat PTA style does not even flicker an eyelid towards the Marquess of Queensberry. The lads stress that the aim of the training is not to be nasty to your assailant; just immobilize the bastard and get out quick: 'Whatever it takes to get him down and make him stay there'; it is amazing what inventive things you can do with an umbrella.

Evasive Driving can be very useful. Just suppose that you are driving down a street in a foreign city. The crowd coming the other way *may* just be interested in teaching you a little Liberation Theology, but do you really want to wait and find out? You could try a hand-brake turn. You need to be travelling at about 30 mph; spin the wheel, accelerator off, clutch down. As the car starts to turn, hand-brake hard on – the car should turn pretty well in its own length; into first and put the pedal to the metal and away! This is just one of the techniques you can learn in Evasive Driving. We spent a happy time on a police skid-pan, to the amazement of some of the assembled constabulary: 'We training ****** joy riders, now?' asked one bewildered policeman. Some advice on skid-pans: a day on them makes you Uncle Dick, and it is also best to practise with someone else's car.

Would you know if you were being followed? Bob took me on an exercise in Kensington High Street. I loitered in door-ways and looked in shop-windows; everybody looked suspicious, but no, I was not being followed. 'Fair enough,' said Bob, 'we'll go back for a de-brief.' By Penguin Books' car park a man was beating up a woman. It seemed only right to escort the lady to the hotel and to a telephone. Bob was inscrutable.

Back in the hotel conference room, we started the de-brief: the door burst open and the Weeping Woman stuck a gun in my ear: 'You're dead, Willy Poole.' I was not, because the gun was a dummy and the pretty lady was Bob's wife, Sue. I had been set up and Sue had been following me all round the High Street.

'You were too soft,' said Bob. I had let a stranger within my 'circle of protection'. A soft heart could get your head blown off: a hard lesson for a hard world.

I can thoroughly recommend the hard lessons that PTA can teach you. The people who seek the firm's training include diplomats, businessmen and others with a high public profile. It should be emphasized, though, that all who travel regularly are putting themselves in a 'risk situation', especially those who travel to the less settled parts of the globe.

Do they offer special courses for women? All PTA's courses are special in that each course is tailored to the particular needs of the customer, or group of customers, and is costed accordingly. The training is not cheap, but you are paying for the best, and what you learn could change your life, or save it.

Chapter Fifty-two

# WOODS, WIZZ AND GRASS PARKS

ONE OF THE pleasures of spending many hours in the woods being very still and very quiet is that the life of the woods goes on around you. You may see the sparrow hawk heading home to feed its brood, with the corpse of a blackbird dangling from its talons. A juvenile wren considers a camouflaged man sitting in a clump of bracken quite the most fascinating thing that it has ever seen. It spends half an hour flitting from stem to stem, whilst it surveys this phenomenon at close quarters and from every angle. The lonely vigil by a pile of sun-warmed stones is cheered by the jolly little lizard (I do not know what kind, I am weak on lizards) who comes out and sits beside the watcher. But this next happening caps everything and if you do not want to believe it, then I give you my absolution now.

It was just on the darkening at the end of October. I was standing behind a tree at the edge of the wood, watching for a roe buck who had been feeding on some young rape. There was a rustle in the fallen leaves behind me. I got a glimpse of movement: 'a dog', I thought, and turned my head. Two little does had come up behind me (upwind!) and were investigating me. One was actually sniffing my rifle butt. I turned my head a little more and she backed back to her sister; the two of them regarded me gravely for what seemed a long time, then they both turned and trotted away, having decided (quite rightly) that I was harmless. The poachers have been active with lamps and lurchers through the summer. Those of you who regard poachers as romantic figures have never met the real thing on a dark night. It is likely that the mother doe had come to a sticky end and that the twins were orphans, which would account for their small size and lack of caution. I shall now keep an avuncular eye on the twins.


There is just a tinge of sadness in the air. You may remember that I sold all my sheep last winter, on the basis that they were meant to help keep me and not vice versa. It was a fiscally sound decision, but something of an emotional wrench; sheep have been part of my way of life for a long time. The blow was softened somewhat by the fact that I let my grazing for the summer, and the farm has been host to five different lots of sheep. Part of the deal was that I was responsible for the twice-daily shepherding round. This gave the collies and me a continuing interest. Now the grazing season has come to an end. A succession of lorries have appeared, and the sheep have packed their bags and gone home. All of a sudden the farm is empty, leaving me with nothing to do but bank the cheque – a pleasing enough activity.

The sheep shed also stands empty, except for the trailer and the gamefowl. It has rather a forlorn feeling. At this time of year we would have been busy setting up the pens, sorting out the plumbing and generally seeing that everything was ready to house the ewes soon after Christmas. I had had it in mind to buy-in some store lambs in the autumn, put them in the shed and bring them up to butcher standard through the winter. I thought better of it. I do not feel inclined to dip my spoon into the agricultural stew at the moment; not with Gummer, McSharry and Uncle Tom Cobbleigh all arguing over the recipe, stirring different ways and very likely picking their noses over the pot as well. I shall wait and see what happens to lamb prices in the spring and then have a think. Until then I shall keep my hands and my money in my pocket and wander my empty acres. It does seem strange, though.


Like some humans, some dogs object to being done good to. Oz, my Australian sheep dog, is a wonderful patient. I can stick needles into him, dress his wounds, remove foreign bodies from his feet; he will take it all with a stoic calm, licking my face afterwards.

There is nothing of the stoic about Wizz, the Border collie. She strongly objects to any form of medical intrusiveness. Treatment normally needs two persons and a muzzle.

I was doing a repair job at the top of the farm the other day when I became aware that Wizz was sitting quietly behind me. This is unusual because she is usually busy in the wood, or digging ineffectually at a rabbit hole. She was just sitting and looking at me. So I looked more closely at her. Somewhere she had picked up a length of rusty barbed wire, and had got it comprehensively wrapped round her and twisted into her thick coat. It would have to be cut away. I could have taken her back to the steading and summoned the para-veterinary task force, except that I happened to know that it had gone shopping and to have its hair done.

Treatment would have to be summary and solo. I took out the dagging shears that live in the box on Henry the Honda and addressed the patient: 'Now you old bisom, hold still, or one of us will get hurt.' The patient thumped her wired-up tail. Kneeling down, I began to snip here and snip there, pulling the wire away very carefully. Wizz sat like a rock, then rolled over so that I could cut away the wire under her belly. It took several minutes to cut the whole length away and the bitch never once complained. At last it was done. Wizz shook herself, did a little dance of delight, put her paws on my shoulder and licked my face. I wish my other womenfolk were always so grateful, but at least they do not have halitosis and muddy paws.

# Chapter Fifty-three

# THE POLITICAL CORRECTNESS OF ZAPPING GREY SQUIRRELS

IT WAS BEFORE dawn when I crept into the shelter of the beeches. The morning was still and knife-sharp with frost. The sheep in the white-rimed field beyond were a huddle of dark shapes. The occasional husky ovine cough was the only sound in the dark. The eastern sky became pink and then red, and things began to take shape in the grey light. One or two of the ewes got to their feet, and the two tups were immediately about their business in spite of the cold. I admired their enthusiasm as I huddled closer into my coat.

The light increased, and there was a flicker of movement in one of the trees. The red squirrel stopped and looked at the strange shape below with its head on one side. The shape seemed harmless; as indeed it was, just very cold. I forgot about the cold and watched the delightful little animal as it scuttled, leaped and climbed in the trees around me. Vertical climbs and descents and beautifully balanced trapeze work kept me fascinated until it was time to head home for breakfast. There had been no sign of the does that I had been waiting for, but the red squirrel made the morning.

I wonder how many people have seen a red squirrel in the wild? They are extinct in most of England except for isolated pockets of population, and their last remaining stronghold in Northumberland and Cumberland. The red squirrel is an indigenous inhabitant of the English countryside. Like so many other aborigines, the red squirrel has been driven from his ancestral home by incomers: in this case that nasty, destructive little immigrant, the grey squirrel.

The grey squirrel might be more properly referred to as a 'tree rat'. It is an American importation, and has no right to be here at all. Many people go 'Oooo!' and 'Aaah!' when they see these horrid things running up and down their bird tables, but they could do the same with red squirrels and with much more justice. The red squirrel does no harm to anyone. The grey squirrel is a destructive animal. It will play havoc with gardens and little trees. Before you think how much you would like to cuddle one, remember that their resident ticks can give you a nasty sort of undulant fever. In most of England the greys have driven out the reds, and now they are threatening the last northern stronghold.

What can we do to Save Our Squirrels? The answer is quite simple: we have to control the spread of the greys.

'Control' and 'manage' are 'Conservationspeak'. They are comfortable euphemisms for the only four-letter word which Conservationists dare not utter: the word is 'kill'. Killing certain animals is an unavoidable part of old-fashioned, lower-case conservation, but just try getting a 'capital C' Conservationist to admit it, and see how they squirm. There was an interesting case in point.

There was a large estate in Scotland. The Royal Society for the Protection of Birds and sundry other Conservation charities tried to persuade the Government to buy the estate and turn it over to them; or, as they preferred to put it, 'to the nation'. The worthy aim of the Conservationists was to preserve and regenerate the indigenous woodlands on the estate, which were under threat. The threat came from overgrazing by red deer. The Conservationists wished to solve this problem by 'controlling' the deer to a level where tree damage became insignificant. This would have meant the killing of a great number (certainly hundreds) of deer, and this was not an isolated operation. If the Conservationists do manage to create a cervine vacuum, then it will be filled by other deer moving in; to be 'controlled' in their turn.

This must be something of a moral dilemma for the Conservationists, but the crunch had to come. They have lived in Beatrix Potter-land too long. It is time that they faced up to the realities of Nature. One of these realities is that to save

Squirrel Nutkin, the northward march of the tree rats will have to be halted. There will have to be a massive 'controlling' of grey squirrels. This will be good for trees, red squirrels and conservation.

At a recent wedding reception, a friend asked me where I and Mrs P. had gone for our honeymoon. What we had planned was a two-week gastronomic tour of Brittany, and we set off in high hopes and a small motor car.

The first night was spent in a vast tower-block hotel in Southampton. The hotel was heated to some ninety degrees. A wedding night is not meant to be spent clawing desperately at an unopenable window.

Within forty-eight hours of landing in France, I was struck down by a stomach bug of such intensity that evacuation became imperative. I wanted to die in England. After an exceptionally active night, the sight of a huge Frenchman with his napkin tucked into his collar, guzzling a whole terrine and slurping Muscadet, gave me a new sense of purpose; and this was when I thought that I had given my all for France.

The little cottage in Gloucestershire was a blaze of light. The friend who was caring for it was doing so by having a party. One half of the bit of the party that had overflowed into our marriage bed was Polish. He was very correct and attempted to click his heels. This is not an easy thing to do when naked, but I am sure that I appreciated the effort.

Chapter Fifty-four

# THE STIRRING TALE OF
# JONATHAN BROCK AND THE
# WOMEN'S INSTITUTE

I FOUND A PHOTOGRAPH of Jonathan the other day. It must be more than thirty years old. In the picture Jonathan is playing with the terriers on the lawn. At that time he would have been about the size of a large grapefruit, but black and white, of course. Jonathan was a badger. He was only about tennis-ball size when I first saw him, curled up in some hay in the bottom of a cardboard box; he was an orphan.

'You take him and welcome,' said Sid, 'I doubt but he'll die though. He's too young to lose his mammy.'

My poor father had had a basinful of youths who came home with cardboard boxes full of things that walked, wriggled or crawled. He expressed himself forcefully and succinctly, then went in search of remedial whisky with the Parthian shot that 'it' was to be gone in the morning. Then mother peered gingerly into the box: 'We had better do something about its fleas,' she said, and I knew that Jonathan Brock had joined the household. To begin with we had to feed him with an eye dropper, but it was not long before he was lapping, and then taking more solid nourishment.

We had been worried about the dogs and Jonathan. The pekes regarded him with some suspicion. It is hard to be oriental and inscrutable when a juvenile badger is pulling your lovely silky coat. The terriers just seemed to accept him as one of themselves, and as the badger grew older and stronger, they would play and wrestle together. Jonathan liked to go for walks with the dogs, but always he would lollop along with his nose almost brushing my heels, chattering and chittering the while. He also chittered when he wanted to sit on someone, and such was his charm that he even found his way on to father's lap. But what he liked best was to climb up on to my shoulders and drape himself round my neck like a fur. On occasion he would delicately nibble an ear lobe. He was a great nibbler, and he could never resist a bare ankle. It was nothing nasty, or spiteful; just an ordinary common-or-garden sort of nibble, and nothing greatly to worry about — once you got used to it.

At that time my mother was some sort of Queen Bee in the Women's Institute. At regular intervals the family would be cleared ruthlessly from the front of the house and banished to the nether regions beyond the green baize door. A peep into the drawing room would reveal rows of stout Institutors in hats, sitting on the edge of their chairs and with tea cups at the high port, whilst they were harangued by mother. On occasion the strains of *Jerusalem* would penetrate as far as the kitchen where father and I sat drinking our tea in companionable silence.

We were thus engaged one Women's Institute afternoon, when the calm was broken by a shriek full of such pain and horror that father and I shot to our feet. There was a further chorus of screams.

'Good God, boy,' said father, starting for the door, 'can someone be raping the WI?' He stopped with a puzzled frown. '*All* of them?' he said. 'Follow me!' he said.

We doubled up the hall in close order and entered upon a scene of chaos and mayhem. The Flower of the WI was standing on chairs, sofas, tables, anything to get it off the floor. The Flower of the WI was clutching its collective skirt and was raising its voice and eyes unto the hills and appealing for help. In the middle of a circle of smashed crockery and discarded handbags sat Jonathan, chittering.

Badgers are nocturnal, burrowing animals. Jonathan liked being under things. It seems that he must have been taking his siesta underneath the sofa in the drawing room. At some stage he woke up and was suddenly confronted with Bare Ankles!

(Oh Glorious Vision!). Not just any old, odd, scrawny bare ankle, you understand, but a row of the most substantial, the sturdiest, the best-developed bare ankles that the district could produce. This was a veritable Savoy-Grill menu of bare ankles. There can be no doubt that the best and biggest of the selection were the ankles that supported the imposing bulk of Mrs Stuggy.

They say that Mrs Stuggy got her sixteen stones from composed sitting mode (with tea cup and extended pinky) to screaming vertical on the sofa with her skirts held high, all in one flowing movement. Those privileged to witness it still speak of the moment with awe. Mother picked up Jonathan by the scruff of the neck and handed him to me with a basilisk stare.

'It takes a brave man to bolt the WI,' said father, putting Jonathan into the poacher's pocket of his coat, as we exited hastily, 'but just now, I think it might be better if the three of us go for a tactical walk.'

As we set off across the paddock, the slightly quavering opening bars of *Jerusalem* came wafting to us:

'And did those feet . . .'

'Yes,' said father, putting Jonathan down, 'they certainly did, didn't they, Jonathan?'

# Chapter Fifty-five

# INDIAN CLUBS COME UP TRUMPS

It is the practice of European peoples to reproduce as far as possible in their settlements and colonies in other continents the characteristic social features of their national lives ... for more than a century no institution has been more peculiarly British than the social club. ... In the tropical possessions of the British Crown the idea of the Club makes a special appeal to the large number of men who are compelled by circumstances to be separated from their wives and families ... to these, Clubs afford some consolation for the pains of exile and loneliness.

THE GENTLEMAN'S CLUB is indeed a peculiarly British institution. Many began in eighteenth-century coffee houses, where like-minded people were wont to gather.

Through time the clubs acquired their own premises and provided oases where people might retire to eat, drink and be merry with their friends. The hurly-burly of the world was kept firmly without, as were inconveniences such as wives and mistresses. This happy state maintains to this day. Not only in London but in other major cities there are anonymous and largely unnoticed buildings, wherein a chap may find a comfortable chair, a quiet drink and a meal amongst kindred spirits.

As the World Map took on the red colouring of the British Empire, the Empire Builders took with them three things that they regarded as necessary parts of a civilized existence: Cricket, Foxhounds and the Gentleman's Club. As one of the oldest and largest centres of British influence in India, it was hardly surprising that Calcutta proved a fertile plot for growing clubs. What may surprise some is that many of these clubs are alive and well and flourishing in the vibrant Indian city of today.

Mention clubs to anyone who knows Calcutta and it is likely that the person's face will light up and he will say: 'Ah yes, Bob Wright; good old Bob.' And as an Indian gentleman described Bob Wright as the 'King of Calcutta', he must be the starting post.

R. H. Wright, Esquire, OBE, is Secretary of the Tollygunge Club. He is also President of the Royal Calcutta Turf Club, President of the British Overseas Citizens Association, President of the Dr Graham's Orphanage and Convenor of the Association of Presidents of Clubs in Calcutta. A large, moustached man (with a remarkable resemblance to the late David Niven), he roars, rumbles and shouts with laughter. He is respected, loved and admired. He is everyone's idea of a 'Burra Sahib'.

Mr Wright was born in Calcutta, where his father was Police Commissioner. He was educated at Cheltenham and Cambridge, then joined the Royal Engineers and was badly shot up in Normandy. He spent two years with the Sudan Defence Force ('the best years of my life'), returning to India in 1947 to work for Yules, a large company with interests in jute, tea and coal. The firm was eventually nationalized, and Mr Wright took on the management of the Tollygunge Club.

No one would dare ignore his wife, the tiny and beautiful Anne Wright. Anne came to India at the age of one. Her father was in the Indian Civil Service. After school in England and Switzerland, she returned to live in India. She founded the Indian Branch of the World Wildlife Fund and the famous Kipling Camp in the Kanha National Park. She is also an OBE for her services to wildlife.

The Tollygunge is some seven kilometres from the city's centre via the dual carriageway that the Metro has reduced to one lane, part of which is usually flooded anyway. It is not surprising that this causes major traffic jams. Apart from hooting continuously, Indian drivers show little signs of impatience, whilst sitting in a solid block of traffic and pollution. It was explained to me that the average Indian likes to spend as much time as possible sitting down. As a driver, he is sitting in reasonable comfort and getting paid for it.

The daily wait in the traffic block did provide a chance to observe the vibrant commercial life of the kerbside stalls and vendors. There is tremendous poverty in Calcutta, but its commercial vitality is immense. Everybody is making, mending or selling something, even on the pavement, and if they are not doing that they are queueing for the cinema; and why do all motor spare-parts dealers also sell herbal medicines?

The Tollygunge is a green and ordered oasis in the chaos of downtown Calcutta. The club used to have a racecourse, until part of the grounds were chopped off for the new Metro Terminal. The one hundred remaining acres still have a golf course and a riding stables, presided over by a magnificently breeched, putteed and moustached cavalry Havildar.

The old stands have now been converted into a most comfortable accommodation block, which is presided over by the unflappable Jenny Das ('I'm just the face behind the scenes'). Jenny married a Calcuttan in England. They moved to Calcutta. She hated it. The family moved back to England. She longed for Calcutta. Now her husband and children are in England and she is back in Calcutta.

There are probably more white faces to be seen at the Tollygunge than at any of the other clubs. It is a favourite place for visiting businessmen to stay, and a favourite place with Indian businessmen to conduct corporate entertaining.

The splendid main house was built in 1780 by one Richard Johnson. It is still thought to be haunted by the Begum Johnson. The house is built in classic Colonial style, with huge, shady rooms that run the length of the building to encourage the flow of air. The secretary of the club lives in some style in an airy first-floor apartment. A flower-laden verandah looks out over the green lawns and magnificent trees.

Everything at the Tollygunge is done with style and cheerful efficiency. In the office, Wright Sahib appears to be able to conduct two telephone conversations at once, dictate two letters simultaneously, throw biscuits at his three Labradors and shout for the whereabouts of 'Chaudhuri Sahib' ('We call him Pimpernel Sahib; we can never find him').

Mr Pratap K. Chaudhuri is the Deputy Managing Member at the Tollygunge, and a nephew of the Maharajah of Cooch Behar. He is a dedicated Clubman, and was an amusing and charming guide through Calcutta Clubland. He placed himself, his car and his driver at my disposal. Getting about in Calcutta is a challenge. The streets are a chaos of decrepit, staggering lorries, buses and cars, all belching black smoke. Mix in people, rickshaws, motor-rickshaws, people, bicycles, handcarts with enormous loads, wandering cows and more people. Add to all of this the fact that having ripped up roads to build the Metro, the authorities have never yet got round to putting them back. Then just for flavour populate every inch of kerbside with booths selling everything from food to retreaded tyres. Driving in Calcutta is a specialized skill and is mostly done with the horn, which is illegal anyway. All in all it was a relief to turn into the tree-hung drive of the Royal Calcutta Golf Club.

The Royal Calcutta Golf Club is another green and pleasant place, and produces a most excellent breakfast. It is a magnificent building, the wood-panelled walls carrying the list of Championship and Cup Winners. The Indian Open is only ever held there, or in Delhi.

Arthur Pereira is the second most senior member; he is over eighty. A tall and immaculately pressed figure, he knows all there is to know about the club and its traditions. He shakes his head sadly over the relaxation of the dress code (coats and ties are on the descendant), and what he regards as the down-market slide of certain other clubs. It certainly did not look as though that was going to be allowed to happen at the RCGC. This impression was reinforced by the Secretary, Colonel H. M. Lall, late of the 9th Ghurkas, and a man who runs a tight ship.

The club is the fifth-oldest golf club in the world, and the oldest outside Great Britain. There are currently 2,600 members. Membership has been open to women since 1950, but few have joined: 'This is a serious Golf Club, rather than a family club. Indian Ladies are not keen on golf, on the whole.' Neither Mr Pereira nor Colonel Lall seemed too distressed by this fact.

There was a rather sad air about the Calcutta Racket Club. Its own roneod handout begins: 'One of old Calcutta's Monuments is about to wage a battle for survival.' No one seemed quite certain when the club actually started, but it was certainly back in the last century. A photograph of 1898 shows 'a distinguished gathering of Victorian Ladies and Gentlemen' drawn up on the lawn to celebrate the opening of a second racket court. However, in the First World War the club was converted into a latrine for British Other Ranks. In the thirties the membership could not even raise the cash to cement the courts. The centre court with the spectator galleries and the 'spacious lounge' were opened in 1953. The design was done by 'the two young Secretaries, uninitiated in the complexities of civil engineering . . .'. It is greatly to their credit that the premises still stand, but the 'lush, green lawns' have been used as a dumping ground for spoil and rubble from the building of the Metro, whose trains may be heard rumbling underneath the club.

The original Calcutta Club was started in 1882. It seems to have had a short life. The present club was founded in 1907. The club-house is stately and dignified, and the atmosphere of the club complements the building. Bearers in immaculate livery are always on hand (the club staff numbers 250). The position of Bearer at a club is greatly sought-after, and tends to run in families.

Any visiting writer is likely to be marched in front of the Club President for inspection. Mr Bhaskar P. Gupta is a barrister of great eminence and renown. His imposing presence and incisive questioning commanded immediate respect; as did the fact that he was able to wear a three-piece suit in the clammy Calcutta heat.

The library (and reading room) was full of rather grand-looking ladies all reading *Punch* over the top of which they glared at intruders like any true club person. An inspection of the library (in respectful silence) revealed such treasures as bound editions of *Punch* back to 1842, *Notable British Trials*, *Bihar Peasant Life* and *Heartsearch* by Mary Napier: something for every taste.

Ladies have been admitted to the ground floor of the club since 1957, when their annexe was turned into a swimming pool. There is the rather sinisterly named 'Room No. 7' which no man may enter without a lady. Perhaps very few emerge, because there were not many men apparent that night. Mr Chaudhuri and I sought refuge in the Men's Bar upstairs with the genial Secretary, Wing Commander Fernendes.

The membership, which has large business and legal representation, is limited to 3,500, all of whom must live in Calcutta and be over thirty. Was there a waiting list? 'A mile long, old boy.' The club is in a prime city-centre position, which means that parking space is limited. Once he has dropped his precious cargo the driver disappears into outer darkness. He is summoned by a raucous and urgent tannoy call. This works best if the driver is not asleep.

Maureen Wallis has lived in Calcutta for forty-four years. She is the leading light of the Calcutta Ladies' Golf Club. She has won the All-India Ladies' Amateur Golf Championship six times.

The CLGC claims to be the only golf club in the world run entirely by ladies. It is also probably the only golf club in the world with a moving club-house. The club exists on the Maidan, a huge expanse of park-land in the middle of Calcutta, which belongs to the Army. The club is a tenant of the Army, who are very helpful, but one of the conditions of the lease is that the club-house has to be moved every year. The problem is overcome by having the club-house on wheels. One year it is pushed one foot to the east. The next year it is pushed one foot to the west. That is the least of the club's problems. They have to share their nine-hole course with herds of goats and packs of footballers. If the Ladies really get in the rough, they are liable to be run over by a tram. There are only twelve playing members, of which Mrs Wallis is the only European. It seems that Indian ladies are not terribly fond of games. They worry about the sun affecting their complexions.

Chaudhuri Sahib's step was brisker as we entered the Saturday Club, which might be said to have a more Woosterish atmosphere. Its 2,000 membership (list currently closed) is described as 'middle-age group'. It boasts five tennis courts, three squash courts and an indoor swimming pool (shades of Catsmeat Potter-Pirbright). There was a sense of 'style' and 'swagger' about the Saturday Club, which was certainly reflected in the Secretary, Brigadier Mehta, late of the Punjab Regiment. The Indian Army has retained the tradition of truly splendid military moustaches which are so rarely seen amongst our own brave lads these days.

Some of this 'style' may also stem from the fact that this club was the honorary headquarters of the Calcutta Light Horse. The last and greatest exploit of this Yeomanry Regiment was to man a 'Q' ship, and mount a successful raid on German shipping during the last war. This earned them a Victoria Cross and later celluloid immortality as *The Sea Wolves* with Gregory Peck in an English accent. The VC hangs in the Light Horse Bar, which still seems haunted by shades of memorable thrashes, and tends to recall memories of 'never leaving it sober in the evening'. European faces are occasionally to be seen in the Saturday Club, as they offer corporate membership to foreign banks and other large foreign companies. There is also some service membership, although the Army tends to live a self-contained life in Fort William. There was the jolly ex-Gunner who had once commanded a Mountain Gun Battery. One of the battery mules had the endearing habit of removing the seat of any trousers within reach of its teeth. The strategic placing of senior visiting officers was all important. By the time our friend had left the battery the score stood at Mule Eleven, SVOs 0.

The club is famous for its social evenings and Inter Club Sports Competitions, where even Ping Pong is ferociously contested. Whilst on the subject of ferocity, the club is a hotbed of bridge, and hosts the World Bridge Championship with over one hundred competitors from twenty-three countries.

Man may not live by bread alone, but the Saturday Club (like some of the others) operates its own bakery for members. Mr Chaudhuri shot off to get his order before they sold out. The club is also renowned for its food. Members have a choice of 'Western', 'Continental', 'Indian Vegetarian' and 'Indian Non-Vegetarian' menus. It also has a separate Chinese kitchen and dining room. Not all Indian clubs offer quite the same choice. Hereafter is a typical dinner menu: Mutton Kidney Soup or Consommé Julienne; Becty (fish) Normandy or Chicken Chipolate or Chicken Alu Curry and Paratha or Tournedo Othelo; Moka Cream or Cheese and Biscuits. The Raj has left a lingering aftertaste.

Bob Wright of the Tollygunge Club gave me strict instructions about making a courtesy call on the British Consul, and wearing a coat and tie when lunching at the Bengal Club. The Consul was so overcome by the honour of my call that he was quite unable to see me, instead sending out a clerk with a form for me to fill in. However, the Ghurka guard at the gate formed up and saluted very crisply, so perhaps they sensed the importance of the occasion.

The coat proved unnecessary at the Bengal Club, but the luncheon was excellent, with a choice of Indian and European food, including a magnificent-looking steak-and-kidney pie. These culinary delights are prepared on lines of traditional, coal-fired brick ranges, the pride and joy of the head cook, Lukash Gomes, who has been with the club for twenty-seven years. There is also a huge tandoori oven, and a half-room-sized traditional, wood-fired baker's oven.

The Bengal Club is the oldest surviving club (1827) in Calcutta. Colonel Nirmal Sarkar follows in the tradition of ex-military secretaries. A sign outside his office says, 'You cannot change the past, but you can ruin a perfectly good present by worrying about the future': an admirable philosophy for a club secretary. The club was an all-male outpost until 1989. There are now three lady members (one a High Court Judge) out of a membership of 1,000. The majority of the members are businessmen, with a legal smattering.

The club is very proud of the teak-panelled Reynolds Room,

so-called because one of the many imposing portraits is attrib-
uted to Reynolds, which is as may be. The club used to have a
magnificent building overlooking the Chowringhee and the
Maidan. This was sold in 1970 ('an administrative decision');
some members feel that the present premises lack the spacious
grandeur of old. Tiger and buffalo heads hang on the passage
walls. The Calcutta crows find the great spreading horns
handy places to perch: must be some symbolism there.

The Calcutta Cricket and Football Club merged in 1965. The
same pitch provides for soccer, rugger, bicycle polo, hockey
and, of course, cricket. There was a slightly depressed feeling
about the place. The verandah was a muddle of broken chairs
from which the crows were picking the stuffing. Land has been
lost to development, and when the club tried to prevent its
perimeter walls being used for the painting of political slogans,
the pitch was invaded by a Calcutta mob.

Indian sportsmen seem to have adopted some of the bluff
heartiness that I understand to be obligatory at Twickenham
and other such places. It is not one of the more attractive
British exports. The first cricket match of the season (President's XI v Vice-President's XI) was in progress, as we gloomily
inspected the historic photographs in the Long Room, which
were being destroyed by damp. 'Howzat!' came an urgent
appeal from the ground. The answer is probably 'Not out and
carrying gamely on'.

The Royal Calcutta Turf Club (1847, Royal in 1912) is a good
antidote to doubt and uncertainty, with its huge portico and
teak panelling and pillars. Upstairs are the sort of leather
armchairs and sofas that invite repose with dignity, possibly
with something from the *'Fur, Feather and Fin'* series. Should
that pall there are the *Racing Calendar*, bound copies of *Horse
and Hound* and, for real deep-thought-inducement, the *War
Memoirs of David Lloyd George*. The club also has one of the
finest teak and mahogany fitted 'Gentlemen's Washrooms' in
existence. Everything, in fact, for bodily and spiritual comfort.

Racing is a very important part of Calcutta social life, and
causes high emotion; as in the case of the owner and member

of the Turf Club who, on being presented with the Queen's Cup by Her Gracious Majesty, thanked her 'from the heart of my bottom'.

It is probably true to say that all the clubs I visited would have a British reciprocal. They would cover the whole gamut from a suburban rugby club to the more rarefied atmosphere of St James. It would be quite possible to pluck a man from a leather chair in Calcutta and plonk him down in the appropriate leather chair in London (or put a pint in his hand and lean him against the right bar) and, apart from the obvious, no one would notice anything much out of the ordinary. Indian society came with social stratifications already built in. Indians have had little problem adapting to clubmanship. Indian India does not seem to penetrate past the watchman at the club gate. The language and mannerisms of the clubs are still well-modulated, if occasionally eccentric, English.

So how fares the Calcutta Clubman? One could say 'Ek dum tik hai', but the Clubman would be more likely to say 'Absolutely splendidly, old chap'.

## Chapter Fifty-six

# AN ORGANIC RUMOUR ABOUT DIVERSIFICATION

'DIVERSIFY!' CRIES THAT Nice Mr Gummer, his spectacles misty with emotion. 'That is the way forward for farmers: diversification into other business outlets.' The answer to that is 'Up to a point, Minister'; the point being that diversification is often easier to pronounce than it is to implement. Take the case of my friend John Manners.

Since 1968 John has been the tenant of a 350-acre mixed farm at Battlebridge in Northumberland. He is a good farmer, and as hard a worker as you will find. He is also a canny businessman, and long since realized the sense of having more than one cartridge in his bag. So about fifteen years ago he started recycling combine harvesters.

Many farmers are fashion conscious. They like to be seen to have the newest and shiniest equipment. As the good times rolled for farming in the seventies and early eighties, so did ever-newer, more sophisticated and more expensive combine harvesters roll off the production line. Last year's models quickly became obsolete.

There are also farmers (especially those who remember father's stories of the 1930s) who reckon that the best place for money is in their pocket. These men prefer to keep old and trusted machinery going. In the current recession, more farmers are doing the same. One of the problems of thrift may be the availability of spare parts for old machinery. Very often it is only people like John who can supply them. The business has customers from all over the country, and also in Ireland, Cyprus and Malaysia. Sometimes the requests are urgent. For an instance: the man from Avon who rang up at 3.00 p.m. in harvest time, desperate for a spare part for an out-of-production combine; it was with him at 10.00 a.m. the next morning.

It is a simple business. The derelict combines stand behind the farm and are stripped piece by piece. The farm and the combines support four full-time workers and a part-time man in the summer. All in all, it is the sort of success story that Mr Gummer would heartily approve of. Alnwick District Council do not share his enthusiasm. At a meeting in late 1991 the Planning Committee 'authorized enforcement action for breach of planning control'.

There are certain oddities about this situation. John has been trading for fifteen years without a complaint. He is licensed as a Scrap Dealer by ADC, and has been paying rates as such. He claims that he had a meeting with a Council official four years ago, and specifically asked if the Council wished him to take any action over the site. He was informed that no action was required. I should explain that the old combines are arranged in three neat (Battlebridge is one of the tidiest farmyards in Northumberland) rows at the back of a wood. There is something forlorn yet dignified about these ancient hulks. They are well hidden from the public view by the trees, and can only be glimpsed briefly as one comes down the main road. A young plantation will eventually shut off this view.

So wherein lies the problem? The first part of the problem is that there has now been a complaint. It will surprise nobody to learn that the complaint came from a person who had recently moved out from the town. People might express mild surprise that any complaint to a Council was (a) paid heed to, and (b) acted upon with some dispatch. They would be people who have not experienced the diligence and efficiency of Alnwick District Council. This excellent organization bows to neither fear nor favour.

There may be another reason for haste on the part of the Council. It is possible that it hoped to pressure John Manners into applying for planning permission (which they would almost certainly refuse) before the end of 1991. Had he applied for planning permission he might then be in breach of his agricultural tenancy, and the Council's problem might have been solved for them. 1991 was important because of the Planning and Compensation Act 1991, which came into force on 4 January, 1992. This 'precludes enforcement actions against uses which have been in existence for more than ten years'.

I telephoned Alnwick District Council. The spokesman said that the matter was quite simple: the Council had authorized enforcement action for a breach of planning control; the appropriate action had not yet been decided. What about the Government exhorting farmers to diversify?

'This matter has nothing to do with diversification,' said the spokesman firmly. 'John Manners is running a scrap yard.' This reply seems to beg more questions than it answers; like: what is diversification? Why is a 'Combine Dismantling Yard' (John's preferred description) not it? It seems that no one knows for sure.

All over the country, diversifying farmers are finding similar problems. Central Government cries 'Forward!', and Local Government cries 'Back!'. The only people to suffer from this muddle are farmers and their farm workers; but then, who cares about them?

Rumour is endemic in rural communities. Quite how a rumour starts is often a mystery, but once it does start, there is no stopping it. It meanders here and rushes there, all the time getting wider, deeper and gathering force as it flows, until it dies as suddenly as it rose. The great thing is to keep it flowing past, and away from, yourself.

Rumours are one of the drawbacks to life in Tightly Knit Communities. Everybody makes a point of knowing everybody else's business, and what they do not know they make up. The fact is that people enjoy a good gossip, and no one is going to let the truth interfere with a good story. Some rumours are undoubtedly malicious, but on the whole they tend to be celebrations of human weaknesses. These are usually of the flesh, about which country people tend to be fairly tolerant. For instance, Rumour has had me misbehaving with a large number of lovely ladies over the years. Masters of Foxhounds are supposed to, or, at least, in rural mythology they are. All I can say is that chance would have been a fine thing.

I did actually start a rumour once, but only by accident. It is an interesting example of how rumour works. I wrote a piece in a magazine, in which I mentioned that I thought it might be rather fun to have a little deer forest in Scotland. About a month later, at a shepherds' supper, it was a matter of fact that I was moving to Scotland. Then Fred, who helps me out on occasion, was in the mart with some lambs. He was told that I had bought a large farm in Aberdeenshire and that he was moving with me as my head shepherd. This sounded jolly good to me, but better was yet to come. At a Parish Council meeting it was announced (and accepted as fact) that I had inherited 100,000 acres and (wait for it!) two castles in the north of Scotland. There was even a splinter group that stoutly maintained that I had an uncle who was a duke, and that I was in line to cop the coronet. All this was getting really quite exciting, and I waited with anticipation for the next instalment. It never came: castles, dukedom and broad acres disappeared like a puff of smoke.

# Chapter Fifty-seven

# PROBLEMS IN THE BORDERS, AT THE BOTTOM OF THE YEAR

'Now the New Year reviving old desires, the thoughtful soul to solitude retires . . .' After changing the year in the Borders a little thoughtful solitude is very much in order. But my desires do not want too much reviving, thank you very much, and especially not when Mrs Poole has got her eye on me.

In the past, I have touched on the rugged endurance necessary for survival in the Borders in the period surrounding Christmas and the New Year. I am humbled by the stamina of the locals. For instance, take the man I saw out hunting recently. I said that he looked a bit 'eyesy', and he pointed out that he had not been 'hyem' (home), or 'oot of his claas' (clothes) for some fifty hours. Weak and feeble southerner that I am, I make no attempt to compete with the hardy, heather-bred hillmen. Any such attempt inevitably ends in tears.

Take a for instance. . . . Between Boxing Day and the New Year our hunt has a joint meet with our western neighbour. This means that we have two packs of hounds, two huntsmen and two sets of followers, who all come together for the day. This happy event takes place at a snug and jolly little pub that has its being somewhere in a howling waste of heather, rock and sitka spruce. This is the pub where they used to think that 'closing time' was the name of a horse running in the 2.30 at Kempton. It is the sort of place that always has a roaring fire, and is further warmed by the beaming personalities of the Mine Host and Hostess. At 10.30 on the morning of the joint meet there was the added ruby glow of tray-loads of Percy Specials.

The first Percy Special of the day imparts a flow of warmth throughout the system, and makes the offer of a second seem like an absolutely spiffing idea. The Percy Special seems such a friendly, confidential, honest sort of drink. It seems impossible that it might have any harmful effects. The treachery of the Percy Special lies in the fact that it has a delayed action fuse. About half-an-hour after the first gulp, something creeps up, taps you on the shoulder and suggests that common sense may be about to evaporate temporarily. You can drink an awful lot of Percy Special in half an hour. You might well be 'foondered' by then, and when I tell you that the mixture is half whisky and half cherry brandy you will see what I mean.

We had a great day at the hunt. There was a combined pack of seventy-three hounds. The cry in the woodlands was tremendous: 'Man,' we kept saying to each other (as we gave each other nips out of our flasks), 'have ye ever hord (sic) such music?;' of course we all agreed that we had not. Hounds spent all day hunting from the East Wood to the West Wood and then, as it might be, from the West Wood to the East Wood. The two woods are separated by a heather hillside, and connected by a road which just happens to run right past the pub. By dark, hounds had caught six foxes and everybody was in high good humour.

'Ye'll tak a dram, Wully,' said Big Dougal, clamping my right elbow in a grip of steel.

'The man's gey gyesend (thirsty),' said Big Dan, clamping my left elbow. Now they can say what they like about me, but I am ever-sensitive to social pressure and local sensitivities: 'Just the one,' I said. There was a fleeting memory of my wife and her crisply emphasized parting instruction that I was to be back in good time (and order) to attend the Old Squire's Drinks Spotty.

It was quite some time later, after I had sung *The Dosing of the Hoggs* and *Jock of Hazeldene*, that I found myself regarding, in a rather glazed manner, the line of seven (or was it fourteen? they kept shifting) whisky glasses on the table in front of me. Somehow the line never got smaller. I would drink a couple, look up and beam at the assembled company, look back at the table and, lo and behold, there would still be seven glasses on the table; of course, one does not wish to give offence. . . .

It was Fred who rescued me. He understands the power of my wife's hard stare. He tumbled me into the van, drove me back and rolled me out on to the Squire's doorstep.

'My dear old boy, how lovely to see you,' said that admirable man, as I swayed gently amongst the gilded throng in his drawing room. Chunks of drying bog mould were falling from my breeches and my tackety boots had reduced the carpet to an instant quagmire. 'You look as though you need a drink,' he said, whilst deftly unravelling me from the cleavage of a Colonel's Lady, 'but you must promise me, absolutely promise me, that you won't sing *The Dosing of the Hoggs*.'

So that, my dears, is how my New Year period began. I cannot tell you how it ended, because, at the time of writing, it is still in full swing .... Well, that's very kind of you, but I already have one in each hand; well, just a small one with lots of water, then (one does not wish to give offence, you understand).

Chapter Fifty-eight

# LA FRANCE PROFONDE

A S I HAVE described it elsewhere, the Bourbonnais is the heartland of France – 'La France Profonde' – a quiet and secret land of rolling pastures and huge oak woods. Most Brits have never heard of the place; they tend to pass it by on their lemming-like rush to the Dordogne and Provence. The British residents of the Bourbonnais would like this happy state to maintain.

Anthony Burstall has lived in France for thirty-eight years. A tall, distinguished, grey-haired man, he is is well known in French society; he is always described as being 'sympathique' and 'bien élevé': in other words, 'a real gent'. Such distinctions are very much alive and well in Republican France. Indeed, they can be a veritable minefield: 'nuance' is a very French word.

As a younger man, Mr Burstall went to work in Paris for a firm of insurance brokers run by his father-in-law to be. He lived in various parts of Paris. As his three children became older, he bought a second house in the Creuze, an area where the English had been unknown since the Hundred Years War. The business was sold in the seventies, and Mr Burstall retired to a life as a writer and translator. He is writing a book on the Bourbonnais, which is aptly entitled *In the Middle of Nowhere*.

Mr Burstall's other great interest is Staghunting, and he is a *bouton* (member) of the Rallye l'Aumance, which hunts in the huge and beautiful forest of Tronçais. To be nearer to Tronçais he moved to his present house, an amazing 1920s chateau, on a hill-top above the valley of the Sully.

There is no doubt that Mr Burstall is very much part of life in France. He describes his outlook as 'European', and with an

Italian daughter-in-law and a prospective French son-in-law this is hardly surprising. He is sometimes asked why he does not take out French citizenship. His reply is that when he finds genuine pleasure in seeing a French three-quarter touch down a try at Twickenham, then he will consider the matter seriously.

Douglas Ryan has become a French rural legend in two years. I was told of this *Écossais Énorme* who had reduced the whole male population of the village of Diennes Aubigny to stumbling incoherence by introducing them to Scotch Whisky. The legend suggests something hairy, seven feet high and Gaelic; probably with a Lochaber axe. Mr Ryan is mild, chubby, bespectacled and comes from Rugby. The Scotch story is substantially true, but Mr Ryan claims that it was a justifiable reprisal for what the French did to him with Pastis. There seems little doubt that Mr Ryan is well embedded in the local community. It could be said that he had a head start. His wife, Marie-George, comes from a family of prominent local landowners.

Through the seventies and eighties, Mr Ryan had a successful land drainage and plastics business in Northamptonshire. He also developed extensive business interests in France, which brought him fluency in French (despite an irredeemable English accent) and his charming wife. In 1988 Mr Ryan's keen nose whiffled out the scent of troubles to come and he sold his business. There was a family conference. The farm at Diennes Aubigny had just come in hand, so they packed up and moved to France with their flock of pedigree Oxford Down sheep; just in time for the collapse of the French sheep farming industry. Nothing daunts the Ryans. They now have a thriving business selling fine English knitwear; Mr Ryan has the French agency for Northampton industrial boots, and they have the farm. Georgie (15), Hope (14) and Zoe (10) have adapted happily to France and prefer the schools, in spite of the much longer hours (8.00–5.00) and the stricter discipline.

All in all, Mr Ryan is a happy man. He now finds the locals very friendly after the initial suspicion about a foreigner. He says that it is vital for any incomer to learn how French thought processes work: they can be quite different from the Anglo-Saxon variety. But there are many parts of life that remind him of England forty years ago, and the weather and the wine are not least amongst the compensations for exile.

John Wheeler-Hopkinson fixed my knee twenty years ago. He was an eminent Wessex osteopath. Claire, his wife, had (and still has) a successful business in antique textiles, which took her often to France. It became accepted between them that they would one day move to France. In 1990 they did just that. They have come to rest in a little jewel of a chateau, in a hill-top village with superb views across the valley of the Sioule and Allier. The acquisition was not without interesting complications. They had to be vetted by the selling family, and Mlle Pierette, of that ilk, has an apartment for life in part of the house. This presents absolutely no problem. Mlle has been a wonderful friend and an instant passport to local life, not least its food. Mlle was in the hotel business. She knows all the best sources of food and wine. She is a lady of respect.

A splendid luncheon party consisting of Mlle and other local worthies showed how well the Wheeler-Hopkinsons have dug themselves into the local community; if the luncheon went on until 5.00 p.m., well, in France there is always time to talk and time to eat: a very sensible approach to life. As Mrs Wheeler-Hopkinson said: 'It is all a matter of time and space.' There is more of both in France. There was enough of it left to stagger along to Mlle's apartment and drink huge glasses of vodka and orange juice.

The answer to the question 'How does the Brit fit in France?' seems to be 'Very well, provided that he makes the effort to adjust'. In the Bourbonnais they have had little experience of the English since *'La Guerre de Cent Ans'*. French memories are long. You will often encounter the accusation: *'Les Anglais ont brûlés Jeanne d'Arc.'* The correct response to this is *'Bien sûr, mais les Français ont transportés les fagots.'*

# Chapter Fifty-nine

# COARSE SHOOTING

I AM A SHOOT Captain. 'Good Heavens!' I hear you say, 'what sort of creature in the world may that be? Shoot Captain? Nothing like that on my shoot.' That is because you own the shoot and run the thing exactly as you want; or (and it is high time you faced up to the truth) exactly as your Head Keeper wants you to run it. It being a fact of life that many Grand Personages are as frightened of their Keepers as they once were of Nanny.

Shooting has never loomed large in my life. I have never been blessed with acres broad enough to encompass a shoot, and I have always regarded shooting as a moderate sport compared with hunting. Two years ago the shooting on a neighbouring estate was up for letting, and a local syndicate was formed to take the lease. I had gone to sleep in a chair after dinner and when I woke up I was told that not only had I taken a gun in the shoot, but also volunteered to run the thing: to be Shoot Captain.

'Why me?' I asked.

'Because you have got a moustache and a shooting suit,' they said. These seemed to be convincing arguments at the time. My duty is to make the arrangements. The other guns consider it their democratic duty to argue about everything that I arrange. My great advantage is the captain's whistle. In moments of stress I blow it at them until they slink off murmuring mutinously.

Some people may have a mental image of shoots based on pictures in the glossier sort of magazine. They may imagine squadrons of gleaming Range Rovers, battalions of smartly dressed keepers, packs of shiny obedient Labradors; sleek men in smart shooting coats accompanied by equally sleek ladies in Loden capes and felt hats with feathers stuck in them. The imagination may expand over shooting lunches in the Lodge with linen, silver, port and Stilton and cigars and. . . .

Our shoot is not quite like that. It is not a Smart Shoot. It is not even a Rough Shoot. It is a Coarse Shoot. We, the Guns (members), are all farmers, except for our Businessman. We once asked him what his business consisted of and he said that he often wondered the same thing.

There is little sleekness about Coarse Shooters, but we do have certain sartorial standards. Black wellies are a must; all waterproof trousers must be green, and coats with 'Blankshire County Council' on the back are not considered quite the thing. I do try to set an example by having a pair of shooting stockings with 'Bang! Bang!' on one sock top and 'Bugger!' on the other. My suit provides hours of fun for all the syndicate, who like to ask whether I buy my tweed by the acre (there being quite a lot of me to cover). There is one Range Rover, but it does not gleam very much. It is only the mud that holds the rust together, and we all agree that the owner would be very unwise to clean it.

Our wives and sweethearts have so far resisted the urge to come and drape themselves round us in the approved glossy manner. Nor would we encourage it. After all, someone has got to stay at home and see to the stock. The only glamour we have is the lovely lady who brings her rather sleepy springer spaniel to help with the picking up of the fallen birds: it is hardly overworked.

We do have some fairly coarse dogs, whose owners spend a lot of time shouting and whistling ineffectually at them. There is a particularly unruly Labrador. One day it was fastened to its owner's shooting stick by some six fathoms of cable. In the excitement of a drive, it ran round and round in ever-decreasing circles until the owner was neatly swaddled and fell over backwards.

I apologize about the absence of the silver, the Stilton and the snowy white linen. We eat our sandwiches sitting on bales in the barn, and I regret to say that any coarseness that you have detected so far is nothing compared with the banter at luncheon. Nor are things redeemed by the smoothness of the sport. Our sport is wild and sinewy, like our birds.

We have a little grouse moor as part of the shoot, and every August we have a day 'walking up the grouse'. The grouse is called Stanley, and he has lived up there so long that he must be drawing his pension. No one really wants to shoot Stanley. He makes sure that we do not by always getting up 200 yards in front of us and disappearing into the wild blue yonder. The shoot does not rear any pheasants. We talk grandly about our 'testing wild birds' and what a lot of wily old sinners they are. They show little inclination to leave their snug strongholds of whins and briars until the beaters have gone past them, when they get up and fly the other way.

So there we are, nearly at the end of another season. We have not got any smarter and we have not shot many birds, but we have had some proper sport. As one gun said: 'We've had a lot of sport and a lot of laughs, but then, with a Shoot Captain like ours, we've got a lot to laugh at.'

# Chapter Sixty

# CIDER UNAIDED, BY
# M DELORS

I SEE THAT THAT wretched Delors chap has been at the Anglophobia again. He has launched yet another attack on the very bedrock of English life. This time he is after that great English drink: Cider. I know that Cider happens in other parts of the EC, such as Normandy and Galicia, but I do not suppose that the swingeing tax increase proposed by M Delors will worry them very much. The Continentals have come to terms with EC Directives: the politicians accept them enthusiastically and the *l'homme dans la rue* ignores them altogether. This is the secret of life in the European Community and only Britain has not cottoned on to it yet. Our foolish politicos insist on enforcing all EC impositions to the last jot and tittle. Mr Delors knows this. He knows that he has no chance of extracting one centime from Alberique, or one peseta from Pedro. The slightest attempt at such an extraction would result in a bloody riot; heads broken, cars burned and municipal offices sacked. But Mr Delors equally knows that, at a word from Brussels, H.M. Excise men will crawl all over the solid cider makers and extract the very fillings from their teeth, with no more protest than the odd muted whimper. That fact, and the fact that we are the biggest cider producers in Europe, is why this measure is peculiarly anti-British.

I was brought up with cider. Granny Poole had her own cider press. I do not mean that the old lady went out and worked the thing herself. That was done by the men on the farm. I can still remember them screwing down the great press, whilst the apple juice gushed out. I can remember the smell of the crepuscular, cobwebby cider house, where the great barrels lurked in the darkness, waiting to pour the taste of summers past into the jug. I have to say that the taste was nothing to get very excited about. Granny's cider was locally known as 'Torfrey (that being the name of the farm) Razor Blades', and it certainly had an astringent charm all of its own. I seem to remember that it had remarkable diuretic properties.

Cider was (and I hope is) very much part of life in the West of England. It is a fine, healthy, natural drink. I used to know men who drank a pint of cider before breakfast every morning of their adult lives. They claimed it as the glorious specific against rheumatism; probably because they succumbed to cirrhosis of the liver before they had time to get the twinge-ing screws. Cider certainly added colour to their noses.

Cider can make fools of us all. I speak a sort of rough-hewn French that gets me by, but I have to say that when the French get into spate amongst themselves I get lost. I tend then to muse on other things, like whether I might possibly force down another sliver of that excellent cheese. Thus it was recently, at a dinner in the Bourbonnais. After a torrent of French conversation which had left me several lengths behind, my charming neighbour turned to me and asked whether we had much ceeder (sic) in Angleterre?

Mais oui, says I, we have much ceeder in Angleterre. It is made mostly in the west of England. I like it very much, I said, it is often of excellent quality. But, I said, you also have in France the ceeder most delicious, especially in Normandy, is it not so?

It was at this stage that I realized that a wheel had come off somewhere. The table had fallen silent. A silent French dinner table is something to remark upon. My wife's French is much better than mine:

'Not cider, you fool, SIDA,' she hissed across the table. SIDA is the French for AIDS. Do you suppose that M Delors might have made a similar mistake?


A puzzle for you: French again, and another fruity matter. Pear *eau de vie* is commonly offered with coffee. You pour it in your cup, after you have drunk the coffee, and let the warmth go to work on the flavour. A huge bottle of the stuff is put on the table and there is always a large William pear floating happily in the *eau de vie*. How do you get a pear in a bottle? Just pause and consider the problem for a minute. I spent two years worrying about it before I plucked up the courage to ask Madame. She looked at me as only the French can look at a prime English twit.

The answer is beautifully simple. The bottle is placed over a bud on the pear tree and tied in position. The pear then grows inside the bottle. Lateral thinking, I suppose.

Chapter Sixty-one

# TWENTY-FOUR HOURS AT THE SAVOY

W̲E̲ L̲I̲S̲T̲E̲N̲E̲D̲ T̲O̲ Mr Major telling Ms Lawley that he would like to take the Oval Cricket Ground to his desert island.

'What would you take?' asked my wife. I did not hesitate.

'The Savoy Hotel,' I said.

On the whole I hate hotels. Most of them have all the charm of airports. Some five years ago I stayed at The Savoy (The Savoy insists on being *The* Savoy), for the first time, and fell in love with it. Like many others before me, I have come to regard the place as not just a hotel, but as a second home. It is not a cheap home, and it has made no concessions in its pursuit of excellence. It has 202 rooms and maintains a staff of 650, which figure includes over 100 chefs. The telephone switchboard deals with an average of 7,000 calls a day. Every year, its guests consume: 160 kgs of caviare, 9,500 sides of smoked salmon, 52,000 oysters, 100 tons of meat, 600,000 eggs, 8,000 lobsters, 26 tons of butter and 9,000 gallons of cream. You may think that Savoy guests are old-fashioned and politically incorrect feeders, but the diet is balanced by the consumption of 5 tons of vegetables each week, along with 700 loaves of bread and 5,500 rolls.

The wine and spirit stock is valued at around £2,000,000. There are 230,000 pieces of glass and china (exclusive Savoy designs) to aid all this browsing and sluicing, which inevitably leads to the use of 15,000 napkins. These will go to the hotel's own laundry as will the other 50,000 pieces of specially woven linen. The hotel also makes its own soap and mattresses.

There is more, much more, but that is enough statistics for the moment. Statistics are meaningless without the people to flesh them out. This is an account of twenty-four hours in the life of The Savoy and some of its people. I hope that it may help to explain why The Savoy is regarded as a place of excellence, not only by the guests, but by those who feel themselves privileged to work there. We start at midnight, when Thursday night becomes Friday morning.

12.01. The front hall is hushed and empty, with not a guest in sight; the world is left to the Night Staff and Lucinda Buxton from the Press Office, my minder.

Mr Reisner has been twenty-two years at The Savoy and Night Manager for nine. He is a confirmed night person. He managed to persuade the Night Auditor, Mr Williams, to emerge from his office and his flickering bank of computerized ledgers. He also gathered up the Night Concierge, Mr Sallan, and Night Porter, Mr Boyer, to be introduced. The four men had seven nationalities between them. The hotel business is a working example of united nations.

12.30. Lucinda suggests a cup of coffee; in the telephone exchange, of course. Marjan (Dutch, and speaks German and Spanish) and Sherry (Egyptian, and speaks Arabic, French and Italian) are an institution. Their voices and names are known to the Great and the Good, the Famous and the Not So Good. In spite of their invisibility both ladies are immaculately turned out. In their dimly lit world of disembodied voices they become privy to many secrets and confidences, but their discretion is absolute, as is their protection of their customers; warn the ladies about Mr Ratfink and he is not going to get through to you, cajole and bluster though he may.

Sherry writes poetry and with a little persuasion you can get a song with your coffee. Her marvellous sultry voice is Eartha Kitt crossed with Edith Piaf, and her rendering of *As Time Goes By* raises a lump in the throat that definitely needs another cup of coffee.

01.30. We wander through the silent grandeur of the River Room Restaurant with its splendid view of the reflection-lit river; the old muddy Thames with her jewels on. This poetic nonsense is stopped short and sharp by stepping into the main kitchens. The cleaners are in, and the cavernous kitchens are an ants' nest of whirring, scrubbing, polishing, pan-clattering activity. This is the kitchen that is presided over by the great M Anton Edelmann, with his staff of eighty-five persons. This kitchen serves the River Room, the Private Dining Rooms, Banqueting and Room Service, so we are talking something like 1,000 meals a day. It is kept very, very, clean.

Darren Crosby is the night chef. The Savoy offers twenty-four-hour Room Service, and Darren has to cater for every kind of nocturnal gastronomic craving.

01.55. Mr Reisner sets off on his rounds. Mr Reisner obviously loves his work and his responsibility for the vast, sleeping hotel. He does a nightly round of each one of the nine floors. We start at the top and work down. Mr Reisner takes random lock-checks with his master key. The locks on the rooms are computerized. As soon as a guest checks out of a room, the key that he, or she, has been using is automatically cancelled and will no longer fit that room.

We inspect a few empty rooms, from neat singles (£175, including VAT and service) to grand suites (up to £615); all with their own bathroom, of course. Each room is decorated individually, and each seems to have its own *ambience*. Some are wood-panelled, some a reflection of mirrors. Noël Coward's favourite was the really rather amazing Honeymoon Suite on the fourth floor, with its richly canopied bed. It did not look terribly restful, but then it is the Honeymoon Suite. Every floor has its floor-service man on duty. Mr Bouihatane comes from Morocco. He is laying the breakfast trolleys for the guests on his floor with the meticulous care that you might expect after twenty-three years at the hotel.

Still going down we arrive at the Ball Room, where every chair is being vacuumed. We pass the embankment entrance to the hotel: 'We don't use this door much, except for film crews when Liza Minnelli is staying,' says Mr Reisner. You soon get used to throw-away lines like that at The Savoy.

0315. Mr Sallan starts off on his shoe-cleaning round. Beside each pair of shoes in the passage, he carefully spreads a mat. His kneeling pad is then placed in the exact centre. He arranges his apron and kneels. Every item of the cleaning kit is laid out precisely, before he sets to with the polish. Cleaning shoes is an act of reverence for Mr Sallan: 'The Savoy is the best hotel I work for; the best and the last.' We leave him kneeling in front of a pair of cowboy boots and perhaps thinking about his retirement in three years' time. His wife is Greek, and they plan to live on an island in the Aegean.

0345. It is now twenty-two hours since I last slept. Lucinda agrees that a short break is permissible. Her assistant, Sarah Manser, will meet me in the front hall at 0530 sharp: to the minute, mind! No. 516/7 is one of the best suites in the hotel, but there is little time to appreciate it. I just want to crash out, but there is a hand-written note pushed under my door. It is from Marjan and Sherry, thanking me for visiting them; bless their hearts.

0500. The telephone rings, and Sherry's soothing voice is hoping that I slept well, and should she call me again in ten minutes, just in case. . . .

0530. In the front hall are Sarah and Mlle Paola Daudre from the Press Office, Phil, our Happy Snapper, and Mr Sharland, Head Chef of the Grill Room kitchen. Mr Sharland is taking us on one of his regular forays to the meat and fish markets. He does this trip about every six weeks. The hotel has its own buyers, but chefs become good by attention to detail. Mr Sharland likes to keep his finger on the market pulse.

There is little romance about the new Billingsgate Fish Market in the Isle of Dogs. It is a garishly lit and smelly temple to the sale of fish. There are fish of every size, shape and variety. Nothing too esoteric is required for The Savoy customers: turbot, sea bass, brill, sole — that is the sort of thing that they like, and they are suspicious of anything new.

0655. At Smithfield meat market we are supposed to meet Mr Swann, the Head Meat Buyer for The Savoy Group (Simpsons, The Berkeley, Claridges, The Connaught). Wires have been crossed, and Mr Swann cannot be found. Our little party goes up and down the central aisle looking for him. You cannot get away with this at Smithfield. It brings out the 'Cheerful Cockney Sparrer' in all present: 'You get paid for walking up and dahn, do yer'; ''Ere come the man wiv the 'at again' (my trilby). 'Thass a nice titfer, Guv'; 'I bet 'ee's the one wiv the money.' A respectful silence falls as the impressive form of Mr Swann appears. He has worked nineteen years for The Savoy Group. He has no budget: 'quality is more important than price'; his brief is quite simply to buy the best. The annual bill for this comes to about £1.5 million. Vegetarianism has yet to catch on amongst the customers of The Savoy.

0800. You will get no better breakfast anywhere than the Staff Canteen at The Savoy: muesli, cornflakes, fruit juice, bacon, eggs, sausages, different varieties of tea, or coffee. Eat as much as you like and none will say you nay. The staff eat from the same supplies as the guests do, the only differences being that in the canteen you carry your own tray and everything you eat is free. But there is no time to dawdle over a second cup of tea, because at 0830 there is the Housekeepers' Meeting in the office of Miss Rosemarie Zander, the Executive Housekeeper: no one keeps Miss Zander waiting.

Miss Zander is blonde, slim, immaculately dressed and German. She has a quiet manner, a dry wit and a way of looking at you over her spectacles that commands instant respect. The six neatly suited Housekeepers are seated in a row opposite her desk. They sit very much to attention, pens and clipboards poised, as Miss Zander goes through matters for attention: customer complaints, untuned television sets, leaks, faulty lights, expected guests (with any known weaknesses and foibles), dripping showers and (horror!) a smell in the loo of 514: attention to detail is minute.

0850. The Valets' Room — the four valets operate two shifts from 0700 to 2100. Mr Jeannette (Head Valet) was hard at work with his iron and steam pipe, pressing suits. He has been five years at The Savoy, thirty years in the business, and has seen great changes: the job is now 'not so much being a

Gentleman's Gentleman as a Businessman's Aide'. The other valet on duty, Mr Dunkley, moved to The Savoy from another hotel four years ago. He thinks that The Savoy has a better class of customer. It is the pride of The Savoy Valets that they try never to say 'no' to a request: be it fitting a guest up with a pair of cufflinks (they have a drawer full of assorted items) or providing a dinner jacket, even unto shortening a ball gown. Both men are properly discreet about some of their more famous customers, although it is comforting to know that The Savoy is favoured by the 'better class of entertainer — the sort who might read music'.

0915. A quick dash to my room to don the pinstriped whistle. Then to arrive slightly out of breath at the daily 0930 Heads of Departments Meeting in the office of Mr H. Striessnig, Director and General Manager, and a very great man indeed. The Heads of Department are all in morning dress. Problems of administration are discussed. The Night Manager's book (in which all your nocturnal peccadillos are recorded) is declared 'all in order'. The modernization of six bathrooms is to go ahead. There have been one or two repair problems, and a slight muddle at Reception, which is not to happen again. The coming weekend is to be busy: the computer system is to go down for twenty-four hours and Royalty will be attending the *Evening Standard* Awards on the Sunday night. Mr Goetz, Front of House Manager, announces forty-seven arrivals; some VIPs; any guests with known problems or special requirements, and which room each guest has been assigned to.

'At this hotel, even the smallest things matter,' says Mr Striessnig.

10.15. The Savoy sits on a warren of passages, tunnels and cellars. Deep in the heart of this labyrinth lies the domain of Mr Mallon, the Technical Services Manager. He is a man in love with the huge boilers that manufacture 16,000 pounds of steam per hour, his planned new £2-million scheme to run all the air conditioning by steam, his new electrical switchgear (The Savoy is a one-megawatt user). His computerized 'Energy Management System' means that he can control the power and heating in every section of the hotel from his office or, if necessary, from his home in Luton. He has been four years at The Savoy, and says: 'Anyone would be proud to work in a place like this.'

11.10. Time for Purchasing and Miss Gizzi, the Purchasing Manager; small, dark, quick, truly *'multa in parvo'*, and another enthusiast. As I am beginning to realize, The Savoy is full of enthusiasts.

Purchasing is an Aladdin's Cave, if rather a slippery one, as great sea bass in boxes of ice trundle by, followed by boxes of oysters. The Dry-Food Store is rich with the smell of spices. Then there are the huge cold stores. No. 1 contains nothing but oranges; all orange juice at The Savoy is freshly squeezed. No. 2 contains muffins, crumpets, black puddings, potted shrimps . . . the gastric juices are on the march. No. 3 is ice cream. No. 4 is milk and cheese.

These are as nothing to the main fridge where there is fruit and veg. (fresh every day), butter, eggs, mushrooms, *foie gras*, truffles, caviare, smoked salmon, Parma ham, York ham, Christmas pudding. . . . It is all much too much, and makes it hardly possible to concentrate on the Royal Doulton, the Wedgwood, the Royal Worcester, the Rosenthal, the silver cutlery and that special cache of Waterford crystal which may touch only Royal lips. It is high time for a tissue restorer, which brings us very neatly to . . . .

11.55. We are in the American Bar with that doyen of Barmen, Mr Dorelli. Mr Dorelli is a tall, distinguished Roman. He has been at the American Bar for twenty-seven years, and is only the sixth man to hold the post since 1926. The American Bar is world-famous, and the walls are covered with photographs of well-known customers: 'Sadly we have lost a few,' says Mr Dorelli, as we inspect Peter Sellers and Lee Marvin.

The little room behind the bar seems to be mostly taken up with a huge ice machine. The working space of the bar seems surprisingly cramped, but Mr Dorelli says that it is well laid out for speed of handling. Anyone who has seen the American Bar in full swallow will appreciate the importance of that. We inspect Mr Dorelli's stock of whiskies: a matter of great personal interest to me. He is modest about his range, but I suspect most tastes would be catered for. We agree on the superiority of Sour Mash (as opposed to Straight) Bourbon and discuss the efficacy of a glass of *eau de vie* with the early morning coffee. Another vodka and tonic (always with a slice of lime, in the American Bar) does wonders for the system.

12.40. Now there is a chance to visit Mr Goetz in his gallery above the front hall, a superb vantage point. Here Mr Goetz controls all admissions and reservations for the 202 rooms. Although bookings are computerized the system is backed up by Mr Goetz's encyclopaedic knowledge of the personal habits and whims of the regular clients.

13.00. A descent to the less rarefied atmosphere of the Meat Room to meet Mr Swann again; also Graham, Norman and Stan. Between the four of them they have 101 years' service at The Savoy. And what a service it is, when you look at rack upon rack of the finest beef and the best lamb. Every piece is dated with its day of arrival. The beef is hung for four weeks. Whenever possible it is Aberdeen Angus. The lamb is all West Country, and is hung for about six days. Most of the meat comes from eight regular suppliers who put aside the best of their week's kill for The Savoy. Pork comes from one farm in Suffolk and the veal from a Somerset farm: the calves are not crated. The Meat Room is truly a temple to carnivorous triumphalism; if it does not send you off to the Grill Room kitchen in fine fettle then you must be . . . a vegetarian.

13.30. The Savoy Grill is not just an excellent restaurant (two Egon Ronay stars), it is also a unique institution, and I love it. To be invited to luncheon with Mr Sharland and Mr Maresca (Grill Room Manager) has to be regarded as an honour. However, work must come before pleasure. The Grill Room is full to its eighty-five-seat capacity. All guests are greeted by Mr Maresca, with his amazing memory for names. Mr Maresca is one of those lovely men who always make you feel that you are the most important person of the day. He knows the foibles of his customers, and always remembers that I like to sit on the station of that Waiter Extraordinary, Mr Rossetti.

At luncheon-time and dinner-time, the restaurant fills with representatives of the Great, the Good, the Not Quites and the Less So, all shovelling away Mr Sharland's food and delicately slurping the excellent wines produced by Mr Carmona, the Head Sommelier. No doubt several macro deals will be settled before the coffee, and many a character will be carved up as skilfully as the beef.

The Grill Room kitchen is not a big kitchen. The twenty-two staff have an average age of twenty. It is interesting that they are all English, except for two Italians. One of these is Mr Piccoli, who has worked there for twenty-eight years and under four Head Chefs: he is a man of respect. Mr Sharland is only thirty, coming to the Grill from the main kitchens, where he worked under M Edelmann.

The kitchen of a great restaurant working at maximum revs is an awe-inspiring sight-and-sound of highly organized chaos. Waiters stream in and out. The *Sous Chef* bellows out the orders, and answering cries come from somewhere deep in the steam, clatter and bustle around the battery of ovens, hot plates and ranges.

Mr Sharland can stand aside from the bustle. His work has long been done. His presence is felt, but he has time for a glass of mineral water and a talk about his beloved kitchen: how it bakes five different sorts of bread (garlic, olive, walnut, sultana, wholemeal); how it makes all its own sauces; pickles its own mushrooms; the truffles at £345 per kilo. . . . He sees it as his pleasure, and his duty, to give his customers what they want: fine traditional food. They eat a hundred oysters, eight sides of smoked salmon, ten saddles of lamb and fifteen pounds of spinach every day. They eat three huge steak-and-kidney puddings every Tuesday, and get through five different kinds of steamed pudding with gusto. Just listening to the man is a gastronomic experience.

A menu of the 1950s has recently come to light. A carafe of claret was 16 shillings (80 pence) and luncheon was 12/6 (62.5 pence). Mr Sharland intends to run some 1950s dishes for a period. He can reproduce the dishes, but not the prices —

caviare was 25 shillings (125 pence): it is now £49.00. However, Grill Room prices have only increased ten per cent in the last twenty years.

We take a break to visit 'Upstairs'. This excellent champagne and sea-food bar is presided over by the genial Mr Ryder. He has the splendid wheeze of selling vintage champagne by the (large) glass, and a different breed every day. It is restful to sip a glass of wine and watch the comings and goings in the main courtyard below; as it might be a party setting off to a wedding. Fine champagne, taken with a now refined hunger, makes one ponder on some of the major philosophical problems of life, such as: why do pretty ladies wear such truly ghastly hats, and why is the Bride's Mother not crying?

14.30. At last, at last, we come to luncheon. We sit at a table in the corner of the now almost empty Grill Room, where a handful of well-fed lunchers are lingering over their coffee and a glass of something to settle the stomach. At last one can tuck the napkin into the collar and let the appetite off its chain.

I suppose that you want the details? Very well, if you insist:

we eat Sauté d'Agneau au Moutarde de Meaux. I do not imagine that my readers will have a problem with that, but just in case, it is sautéd loin of lamb, with aubergine and parsnip mousse, wrapped in a pig's caul, then baked with a jus. It comes with a spaghetti of vegetables and pommes rösti, with the sauce made from the jus from the cooking liquor, cream and Moutarde de Meaux. You do not 'wash down' a meal like that, but the pleasure of good food is immeasurably increased by judicious draughts of good wine. I do not think that anyone is going to argue with Mr Maresca's choice of a Chateau Meyney 1988. I can tell you that it is delicious.

To call the meal good would be tautology, but why not, and good company complements good food. It is a merry meal. Mr Maresca knows my weaknesses, and presses a cigar and a glass of the 1969 Calvados on me; then another one – why not? Mr Striessnig joins us in jovial mood, teases everyone and strides away to make a brief dramatic appearance in the Press Office where he raises his hands to heaven and cries: 'They are all getting drunk in the Grill Room,' exiting to proper public relationship consternation.

1600. Suite 516 and blessed oblivion until 1700. Then it is shave, bathe and into the dinner jacket to parade at the Press Office for the evening shift. That evening there are private cocktails and dinners in Princess Ida, Patience, Pinafore, Sorcerer, Gondoliers and Beaufort. The Private Rooms are all named after Gilbert and Sullivan operas, except Beaufort. Beaufort Buildings stood on the site of the present hotel.

The Private Rooms and the beautiful River Room Restaurant are managed by Mr Zambon. Some nights he sits 400 people down to dinner. He introduces Kaspar, The Savoy's lucky cat. Kaspar is black and wooden and was designed by Basil Ionides in 1926. Should a private dinner party work out at thirteen guests, then Kaspar joins the party at table with his own place setting. There is also revelry in the Banqueting Rooms that night: an offshore bank that prefers anonymity and shuns the intrusion of the Press is having a dinner dance. So are the Royal Free Hospital Nurses, about whom there is absolutely no secrecy.

1830. Mr McKenzie is standing watchfully by the Banqueting Entrance. He is the Security Manager, and heads a staff of ten. Royal and diplomatic visits are his main headache, and he has close relations with the merry men of Bow Street nick. It hardly needs saying that security is very discreet at The Savoy. However, should you decide to visit wearing your spider's-web tattoo and nose rings, you would very quickly find yourself being asked politely if you are in need of help to return whence you came.

1920. Now for a much-needed stiffener at the American Bar. The bar is packed, and the singer/pianist is being smoochy. The atmosphere and the clientele are about as close as The Savoy gets to loucheness; which is not really very. Mr O'Connell is in a dinner jacket and alert attendance. He is the Food and Beverage Manager. His poker face conceals a ready Hibernian wit and a mind with computer-like qualities.

2010. Banqueting is overseen with robust efficiency by Mr Downer, the Banqueting Manager, and his assistant Mr Harvey. They are very street-wise young men, with razor-like wits. These are necessary qualities when dealing with large numbers of people who are intent on allowing their common sense to evaporate temporarily. This is especially so when you consider the sheer scale of the operation. Banqueting serves over 130,000 places per annum. Just consider the logistics of the Nurses' Ball: 380 guests at thirty-six tables for a three-course meal (smoked salmon, chicken in lemon sauce, blackcurrant mousse and sorbet), thirty-six waiters, fifteen wine waiters, and probably some 200 bottles of wine, amongst other beverages. The dinner and dance takes place in the Lancaster Room. This room is very Savoy, with splendid ornate plaster work and a ceiling painted with white clouds and blue sky. Huge wall mirrors reflect the candle-light and the glamour of the occasion. You can understand why the nurses return year after year.

The nurses and their consorts are in spate arrival and high excitement at the prospect of a night away from the bedpans. One unfortunate lady has broken the heel of her shoe in her excitement. With Savoy smoothness, Mr Downer finds her a temporary pair and sends the broken shoe to Technical Services, where the duty electrician promptly mends it.

In the Banqueting kitchens it is organized chaos time, with milling waiters, scurrying wine waiters and a Babel of languages from Hungary, Egypt, Italy, Spain and more ('For God's sake don't call the Thais Chinese; it makes them nasty'). Space is limited in the service area, and a one-way traffic system is in operation. This is designed so that those with laden plates do not meet head on those with expertly, but precariously, balanced piles of empties. The system is enforced vigorously, vocally and sometimes physically: waiters with the adrenalin pumping take a bit of stopping.

In the room the decibel level is rising. The nurses are tucking in with gusto and the wine is flowing. A medical student makes loud demands for champagne. Mr Harvey moves smoothly to whisper discreetly in his ear that the house champagne (excellent) is £35 per bottle. This quietens him. On the stage a string quartet is struggling against the noise. The dinner ends with the serving of the celebrated 'Savoy Pralines' – ice-cream covered in black and white chocolate, served on a bed of dry ice, which smokes in a most satisfactory manner and makes everyone go 'ooooooo!'

Then it is disco time: *fortissimo* and *con mucho gusto*. Mr Harvey and I watch the gyrations from the door. A generously built nurse swerves towards us: 'You're going to be propositioned,' says Mr H out of the corner of his mouth. But, on closer inspection, the lady decides that her evening is not *that* bad and turns away. The only proposition that comes my way is from the young man in a kilt who asks if I am the bouncer. Even The Savoy cannot work miracles and turn me into a handsome prince. It had worked a sort of miracle by keeping me awake and fascinated for twenty-two hours out of the twenty-four. Upstream, Big Ben is striking 1200. It is time for me to turn into a pumpkin.

One of the Directors of The Savoy once said that the three things that make a good hotel are Service, Space and Style. It is a very simple formula, which The Savoy follows without compromise. That is why it is quite simply the best.

Chapter Sixty-two

# COUNTRY LAW

Dave Dunn was yawning a bit. He had been up all night shadowing a team of poachers, until they had been manoeuvred into the welcoming arms of the constabulary. It was a misty Sunday morning, and we were bumping along the Ridgeway near Wantage. The mobile telephone bleeped, and a crackly voice said:

'Gordon here; we've got coursers on the farm.'

'Roger, Gordon; we'll be with you in about ten minutes.' Dave spun the truck round, and we crashed and bumped along the rough track. As we drove, Dave talked into his CB radio, alerting the local gamekeepers.

Farmer Gordon Pill met us at the bottom of the hill. He had two farm workers and his gamekeeper with him. Two game-keepers from the next-door estate arrived, one muttering that he had had only one bite at his Marmite sandwich when the alarm came. You may think that there were quite a lot of us, but illegal hare coursers are not well known for verbal or physical reticence. The police had been telephoned.

We gathered in the strip of trees beside the road. One field away, two men were walking across the plough with lurchers on leads. A battered estate car was keeping pace with them on a farm track. Dave shinned up a handy conifer. The poachers were hull-down on the plough. So far they had done nothing more than 'just walking the dog, Guv'. We waited.

'Right! there's a hare up! they've slipped! let's go!' Dave came down the tree in a way that made my eyes water.

We raced round and up the track, blocking the estate car, the driver sounding his horn frantically. One man managed to catch up his dog, but the other dog was well locked onto its hare. Hare and dog disappeared into the scrub at the far end of the field.

Kevin, Wayne and Doug were the soft-end of the illegal coursing business. They were cheerful rogues out for a bit of sport at someone else's expense.

'You rotten buggers coming and catching us.'

'I think I'll get a poodle – lot less trouble.' Doug appeared having retrieved his dog. The hare? 'What f— hare? This f— dog catch a f— hare? You got to be f— joking.'

Dave and the keepers have no powers of arrest. Once the three men had given their names and addresses they were free to go, and there was no sign of the police. Dave kept them talking, boasting about their dogs and how they would be back again next week. They told us that they were good poachers: they never poached deer, or cut fences, or ran their dogs near in-lamb ewes. A constabulary Land-Rover came bumping down the track: 'You rotten bastards keeping us talking.'

The constabulary took what may or may not have been three different names and addresses, and cautioned the three. They had been caught, *in flagrante*, in breach of Section 30 of the Game Act 1831 (trespassing in pursuit of game). They were very relaxed about it. They knew, we knew and the police knew that the chance of such a case finding its way into the overloaded court system was minimal. We all knew that they would be back next weekend.

These lads were the blunt end of a much nastier problem. The rolling open downlands of Berkshire and Hampshire are well stocked with hares and are ideal coursing grounds. Easy motorway access and 4 × 4 vehicles bring urban gangs with their dogs. There may be forty or fifty men. They just sweep across country. They cut fences and drive across crops. These men are accustomed to physical violence and intimidation. Their activities have nothing to do with sport, and everything to do with telephone-number betting.

So desperate had the situation become that eighteen estates banded together and called in Dave Dunn. Dave Dunn runs Countrywatch (UK), specialists in farm and estate security. Dave served in both the New Zealand and British armies, and then the enforcement branch of the NZ Wildlife Service. He emphasizes that Countrywatch is not a vigilante organization: its operatives always work strictly within the law and in liaison with the local police. Countrywatch operatives are skilled in surveillance techniques. Violence is avoided and talked down whenever possible.

Norman Carlisle farms 2,000 acres on the downs. His problems have increased dramatically over the last eight years. He has been threatened by gangs, his fences have been cut, his ewes scattered and 'New Age Travellers' have squatted on his land. Things are so bad that he dare not leave the farm for a day. He is an enthusiastic client of Countrywatch.

For the rest of the morning we quartered the area. There was one report of coursers, which turned out to be mistaken. Dave seemed rather disappointed. He said that every weekend until recently there had been at least three major incidents, most of which had been successfully intercepted.

We got out the 'Spy in the Sky'. Besides farming, Gordon Pill builds 'Thrusters', Australian-designed, two-seater microlite aircraft. He often does aerial reconnaissance for Dave. There was a bit of head scratching as they pushed, squeezed and levered me into the passenger seat: 'The biggest bloke yet'. Microlites take a bit of getting used to (1,000 feet looks an awfully long way down), but they are a marvellous viewing platform. In ten minutes we had spied the whole Countrywatch patch. All was quiet: Countrywatch's efforts were beginning to pay off.

It is sad that Countrywatch looks like becoming a growth industry. There has been a tremendous upsurge in rural crime during the last ten years. Rural vandalism is on the increase. Farm thefts and poaching are now highly organized, and big business. The police lack the resources and the expertise to tackle the problem. It must be said that some forces appear to lack the will, as well. Country people may have to look to themselves in future, and to the skills of men like Dave Dunn.


Am I missing the lambing? people often ask me.

1 April was the third day of the worst rain in Northumberland since Noah. My little burn is normally a quiet, inoffensive

little thing, but by 1 April it had disappeared in an inland sea.

I returned from my early morning saunter in the wood for my breakfast, sodden and shivering, to be met by another sodden, shivering man. Artie's lambing field was a field no longer; just a series of shrinking islands in a lake. Was there any chance of my sheep shed? There followed a frenzy of pen-building and leading-in loads of straw.

Then came a shuttle of tractors and trailers with ewes and lambs all in an advanced state of waterlogged misery and hypothermia. All the time the rain teemed down and the floods spread. By night time everybody was in a state of exhaustion, but the ewes and lambs were safe.

That night there were four inches of snow.

Do I miss the lambing? May Heaven preserve your innocence!

# INDEX

abattoirs, EC regulations, 156–7
Agriculture, Ministry of (MAFF), 7, 8, 10, 149
Andrade family, Smithfield, 31–2
Apatu, Margaret and Terry, 26
Appleby Horse Fair, 76–7
Arres, Tom, dyker, 61–3

badger, Jonathan, 183–5
Badminton Conservation Trust, 131–3
barbecues, New Zealand, 23–4
barn owl, meets kestrel, 130
BASC, 119
Bearsports Outdoor Pursuits Centre, windsurfing, 140–2
Bengal Club, Calcutta, 193–4
Blencathra Hunt, 165–70
boar hunting in France, 91–2, 94–5, 96–7
Border, the vii, 43, 110–11
Borders, 'Riding Clans', 33, 43, 86
Bowman, George, 98–101
Bummarees, at Smithfield, 31
bureaucrats, hatred of, 109
Burstall, Anthony, 203–4

Calcutta, clubs in, 187–95; Calcutta Club, 190–1; Cricket and Football Club, 194; Ladies' Golf Club, 191–2; Racket Club, 190
carcases, disposal of, 148–9
carriage driving, 98–101
cattle, at GYS, 49; Charollais (in France), 89; French system of, 90, 93, 94; Galloway, 2, 72; Kylie, 67; Longhorn, 45, 154–5; rare breeds, 153, 154–5; Shorthorn, 48

Certificate of Rural Competence (CRUC), 123
Chaudhuri, Pratap K., 189, 191, 192, 193
Chevallier-Chantpie family, 88, 89–97
Cheviot, name, place and sheep, vii–viii; path up, vii, 152
cider, 209–10
City of London Orienteering Test (CLOT), 123–4
Clark, Peter, 140–2
Clean Boot hunting, 113–15
Clearances, in Scotland, 67–8
clothing, advertisements for, 163–4; large American, 173
clubs, Calcutta, 187–95; London, 14, 186–7
committees, 38, 151–2, 197–8
common rights, 116–17
conservation, awards, 39–41
Conservationists, 181
Coquet valley, 42–3
Countryman, Indigenous, 68–9
Countrywatch (UK), 226–7
coursing, illegal, 225–7
crows, EC protection for, 129–30
Cubby, John, 119, 120, 121

Davies, Ron, MP, 108–9
deer management, 119–21, 181
deer, red, 120, 181; hill stalking, 162–3
deer, roe, French cull, 92–3; observed, 109, 122–3, 177–8
Delors, M Jacques, 209
Derwent Hunt, 39–41
dog shows, 4; NZ hounds, 22–3
dogs, bloodhounds, 5, 113–15; bull-dogs, 4–5; docking of tails, 150–1;

Dogs (*contd*)
  Jack Russell as breed, 4–6; for mink hunting, 56; neurotic, 158; Rottweilers (Duncan), 3–4; sheep- (Oz), 148, 178–9 (Wizz), 179; telepathy in, 2; unruly Labrador, 207
Dunn, Dave, Countrywatch, 225–7
dykes *see* stone dykes (walls)

EC directives and regulations, on abattoirs, 156–7; and carcase disposal, 148–9; on cider, 209; on crows, 129–30; on fishing industry, 128–9; proper attitude to, 129–30, 209; stock in transit, 28–9
eggs, free-range, 7–9
elephants, 80, 82–3, 83–4
enclosures, and demise of English peasant, 116–18

farm machinery, 50, 196–8
farming, conservation and, 39–41; decline of, 68–9; and diversification, 196–8; in France, 88–97, 117; in New Zealand, 23; part-time, 10–12, *see also* fish; wild boar
Farming and Wildlife Advisory Groups (FWAGs), 39
farms, prices of, 160
field sports, Labour Party and, 108–9; and New Sportsmen, 64–5
fish farming, mussels, 146; oysters, 145–6; salmon, 144–5
fishing industry, and EC, 128–9
food hygiene, a robust attitude, 118
Fordley Hall Country Sports Course, 65–6
fox hounds singing, 150
fox hunting, 37, 157–8, 200; Blencathra Hunt, 165–70: in the Borders, 85–6, 111–12; in France, 95; uncanny tales of, 73–5
foxes, and game fowl, 135, 171–2; gassing of, 108–9
France, 117; Bourbonnais, 88–97, 203; British residents in, 203–5

game fowl, 19–20, 129; taken by foxes, 135, 172
gassing of foxes, 108–9
Germany and the Germans, 36–7
Ginger, game cock, 19–20, 135
Great Yorkshire Show, 45–51
Grizedale Forest, 119–21
grouse, Stanley, 208
Gummer, Nice Mr (John Selwyn), 7, 10, 129, 149, 196
Gundry, Major Gerald, 74–5

Hare, Robin and Maggie, 64–5
hare(s), chased by roe doe, 122–3; plentiful, 134
Harrington, Earl of, 73–4
Harris Tweed, 125–7
Hawkes Bay Hunt, 21, 22, 23–4
hedges, and enclosures, 116–17
hens, and salmonella, 7–9, *see also* game fowl
Hill, Robin, 74
honeymoon, author's, 182
horses, Appleby Horse Fair, 76; at Great Yorkshire Show, 45–6; breaking, 103–4; carriage driving, 98–101; Dobbin and plough boy, 20; Nunnington (Household Cavalry), 102–7; and point-to-points, 17–18
Household Cavalry, Black Horses (Nunnington), 102–7
houses, author's Single Storey Dwelling, 87, 161; heating of, 86–7; for local people, 68; in Northumberland, 159–61
Hutchinson, Tot and Anne, 58, 59

India, 79–84; clubs in Calcutta, 187–95
Indigenous Countryman, 68–9

Jockey Club, 16–17
junk mail, 147

Kanha National Park, India, 80–2
Kennel Club, 4, 6
Kipling Camp, Kanha National Park, 81, 187
Kipling, Rudyard, 80–1

kippers, undersized, 128

lambing *see* sheep
Langham Primary School, 132–3
Lewis, Isle of, Harris Tweed, 125–7;
  kippers, 128–9
Little, Matt, 33
London, 4 × 4 vehicles in 172–3;
  Countrymen in 13–15; transport to
  and in, 14–15, 123–4

magazine advertisements, 163–4
magpies, EC protection, 129–30
Manners, John, 196–8
markets, in France, 95–6
Mead, John, 154, 155
memory, modern loss of, 1–2
microlite aircraft, 227
mink hunting, 55–7
mussels, 146

New Sportsman, courses for, 64–6
New Zealand, 21–6; Hunts' Association,
  21
Ngamatea farm, Hawkes Bay, 24–6
Nunnington, Black Horse, 102–7

otterhounds, mink hunting, 55, 56
oyster catchers, on pond, 28, 134
oysters, farmed, 145–6

paratroopers, Belgian, 43
Peakes Covert, 132–3
pears, in *eau de vie*, 210–11
peasants, demise of, 91, 116–18
peat cutting, 33–5
Peel, John, 165
Percy Specials, effects of, 201–2
pigs *see* Rare Breeds; wild boar
Pinder, Chris, 137–9
poachers, 177–8, 225–7
point-to-points, 16–18
politicians, and rural vote, 10, 69, 116–
  18
pond, dew, 40; digging of, 27–8;
  features of, 134–5
Protection Training Assessment Ltd,
  174–6

Quangoroos, 151–2
Queen Elizabeth the Queen Mother,
  honorary Bummaree, 31

Ramblers' Association, 162
rant, tirade or tune, viii
rare breeds, 59, 153–5
Rare Breeds Survival Trust, 153–5
ratch, to (verb), 171
Royal Army Veterinary Corps, 102
Royal Calcutta Golf Club, 189–90
Royal Calcutta Turf Club, 194–5
rumours, how they work, 198–9
Russell, Parson Jack, 5
Ryan, Douglas, in France, 204–5

St Kilda, weather forecasts, 2
salmon, farmed, 144–5
salmonella, and hens, 7–9
Saturday Club, Calcutta, 192–3
Savoy Hotel, The, 15, 212–24;
  administration, 217; American Bar,
  218–19; at night, 213–15;
  Banqueting, 223–4; boiler rooms,
  217–18; Housekeepers, 216; kitchens,
  214, 220, 224; Private Rooms, 222;
  purchasing, 215–16, 218, 219;
  reservations, 219; rooms at, 214;
  Savoy Grill, 219–22; security, 223;
  shoe cleaning, 214–15; valets, 216–
  17
Scotland, and the Clearances, 67–8, *see
  also* Lewis, Isle of
Scouts, 52; Les Scoots, 53–4
self-protection, 174–6
Sharp, Mrs, free-range eggs, 7–8
sheep, author sells, 68, 178, 228;
  Cheviot, vii; cowing, 36; in France
  91, 93; lambing in bad weather,
  227–8; mothering-up, 135–6; New
  Zealand, 25, 26; rare breeds, 154,
  155; shearing displays, 50–1; stock
  records, 1; to the slaughterhouse, 28,
  156–7
shepherds, and fox hunting, 85–6; stock
  records, 1–2
shoot captains, attributes of, 206, 207

shooting, coarse, 206–8; courses for game-, 65–6; tests for, 123
shows, agricultural *see* Great Yorkshire Show
smallholdings, 10–11
Smithfield Market, 30–2, 215–16
snow, 2, 72, 172–3
spring, in the Borders, 19–20, 134–5
squirrels, red ousted by grey, 180–2
stalking *see* deer; deer management
sticks, 50
stone dykes (walls), 61–3
Stoneleigh, Rare Breeds Survival Trust, 153–5
stones, 61
suburbanization, viii

telepathy, dogs' use of, 2
thatching, 49
Threlkeld, Blencathra Hunt at, 165
threshing demonstration, 58–60
tigers, 83
Todhunter, Barry, 166–7
Tollygunge Club, Calcutta, 187–9
topping pastures, 147–8
travel, in India, 79–80, 187–8, 189; in and into London, 14–15, 123–4
Trooping the Colour, 105–7

trotting races, Appleby, 77, 78

vehicles, All Terrain, 147–8; four-wheel drive, 172–3

weather, in Borders, 157–8; forecasting, 2, 70–2
weaving, Harris Tweed, 125–7
West Yorkshire Mink Hounds, 55–7
Wheeler-Hopkinson, John, 205
wild boar farming, 137–9, *see also* boar hunting
wildlife and conservation award, 39–41
Windsor Forest Bloodhounds, 113–15
windsurfing, 140–2
winter, weather prospects, 70–2
Women's Institute, and badger, 184–5
Woodland Stalking Course, 119–21
woodlands, life in, 177–8; management, 131–3
Woyka, Captain Valentine, 102, 104
Wright, Anne, 81, 187
Wright, Bob (R. H.), Kipling Camp, 81; Tollygunge Club, 187, 188–9, 193
Wykes, Nick, 30

Yorkshire, FWAG awards, 39–41